Jean QUELLIEN

Landing Beaches

OREP

EDITIONS

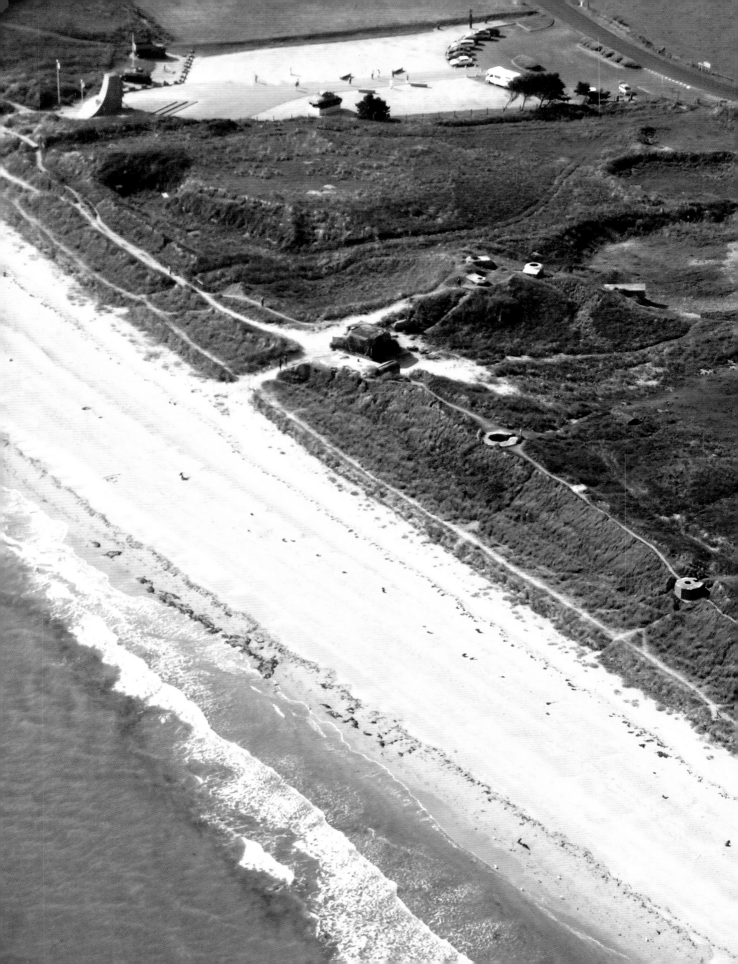

Contents

From Dunkirk to the Normandy Beaches

DUNKIRK, early June 1940. An unbelievable noria of ships of every imaginable size managed to evacuate the nearly 350,000 British and French soldiers who were trapped in a narrow pocket on the North Sea coast following the lightning German offensive that had been launched three weeks previously. At that tragic moment, when Great Britain was to find itself facing the triumphant Wehrmacht alone, the Prime Minister, Winston Churchill defiantly threw down the gauntlet, saying «We'll be back!»

The Genesis of Overlord

Almost exactly four years later the British were indeed to set foot on French soil again, in Normandy, in the company of Americans and Canadians on a certain 6th of June 1944. The route from Britain to Normandy turned out to be much longer than the actual distance separating them might have suggested. It was also more tortuous. Of course, the USSR's entry into the war in June 1941, then America's in December of that same year put an end to Great Britain's isolation, but it was still necessary to find agreement on strategy.

The British urged caution in the face of the impatience of the Soviets, who were clamouring for the opening of a «second front», and the Americans' desire to lose no time in attacking the Third Reich directly, in order to enable them to move against Japan as early as possible. The British advised attacking the Reich's periphery, with the aim of weakening the adversary before delivering the fatal blow. The tragic outcome of the raid on Dieppe in August 1942, which cost the lives of over a thousand men, indisputably confirmed Churchill's contention that an amphibious assault on the coasts of occupied France would be very premature. So, like it or not, the Americans were constrained to accept the British strategy that led the Allies to land first in North Africa in November 1942, then in Sicily in July 1943 and finally in Italy two months later.

In return for these concessions, the question closest to their hearts was put back on the agenda: the great cross-Channel offensive. The principle had been agreed upon in Casablanca in January 1943.

■ Winston Churchill was the perfect embodiment of British tenacity.

■ The raid on Dieppe
Operation Jubilee, launched on 19th August 1942, was a gory fiasco. Around 4,000 men (mainly Canadians) were killed, wounded or taken prisoner.

■ Eisenhower and Montgomery surrounded by the Overlord general staff

During the Trident conference, which took place in May in Washington, the vast landing project that had been presented by the Americans as early as spring 1942 under the code-name «Round up» was brought back down off the shelves where the British had left it and re-baptised «Overlord».

The exact location of the assault had yet to be defined. The Quadrant conference, which took place in Quebec in August 1943, decided it should be on the Seine Bay coast rather than in the Pas-de-Calais, the latter being judged too predictable a choice with regard to the Germans, because of the shorter distance the assailants would be required to travel. The date settled on for the launch of the operation was the beginning of May 1944.

The slowness of their progress in Italy merely reinforced the Allies' need to concentrate their efforts on the preparation of Overlord. The American General Eisenhower, who stepped in as Commander-in-Chief in December 1943, and his deputy, the British General Montgomery, agreed to widen the initial assault sector, which they judged to be too narrow, and to engage larger numbers of troops. This made longer preparations necessary: D-Day was postponed for a month, until the beginning of June 1944

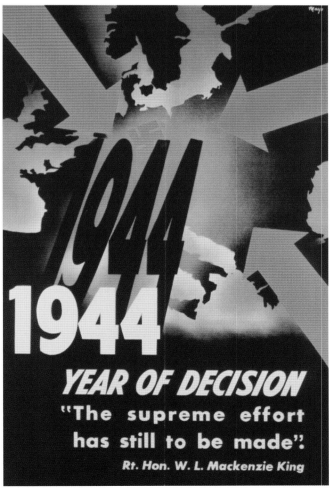

■ Canadian propaganda poster

The Atlantic Wall

■ The Atlantic Wall under construction

Contrary to Hitler's hopes, the brutal offensive he launched against the USSR in June 1941 did not result in a decisive victory. The Red Army, which was at first routed, regrouped outside Moscow in December. Henceforth, the Eastern front was to swallow up a growing number of divisions, obliging the German general staff to make dangerous reductions in the forces on the Western front, under the command of Marshall von Rundstedt since 1942.

Under these circumstances, the fear of an Allied invasion on the French coast, heightened by the United States' entry into the war, pushed Hitler to give the order to begin construction of an impressive defensive system, soon to be known as the «Atlantic Wall», as early as December 1941.

Work indeed began in the spring of 1942, but was not yet complete in June 1944. The scale of the task entrusted to the Todt Organisation was, admittedly, colossal, as it required the construction of around 15,000 concrete structures of varying shapes and sizes. As a consequence of the raid on Dieppe, priority was given to defence of ports.

■ Marshall Rommel on an inspection tour of the beaches

■ The 88mm gun bunker on the sea-wall at Ver-sur-Mer, today converted into a nautical centre

Azeville, Maisy, Pointe-du-Hoc, Longues, Ver, Ouistreham, etc.

Marshall Rommel, who was given the mission of inspecting the Atlantic Wall at the end of 1943 and was immediately afterwards appointed commander of Army Group B charged with the coastal defences between the Loire and the North Sea, quickly detected weaknesses in the system. He gave particular attention to the Seine Bay sector, which to his mind had been neglected in favour of the Pas-de-Calais sector.

which were transformed into veritable fortresses bristling with guns and practically impregnable by frontal assault. Long range, heavy-duty batteries, whose business it was to keep an invasion fleet at bay, were established along the coasts between them. There were thirty or so of such batteries between the fortresses of Le Havre and Cherbourg, notably at Saint-Marcouf-Crisbecq,

On his instructions, concrete pillboxes with thick walls were hastily built to protect the heavy artillery, often situated in open trenches or vats, from aerial bombardment. Above all, Rommel multiplied the smaller fortifications all along the coast, the *Widerstandnesten* (WN) or «resistance nests» equipped with medium bore guns, machine-guns or mortars and whose objective was the close-range defence of the beaches against assault troops. The shores themselves were covered with all sorts of obstacles, designed to rip the bottoms out of landing barges or to blow them up.

However, he did not receive permission from the Wehrmacht top brass to station armoured divisions near to the coast in sufficient numbers to be able to repel the Allies back into the sea through vigorous counter-attack. He left his headquarters in La Roche-Guyon on the 5th of June with the firm intention of persuading the Führer to grant him this authorisation... only a few hours before the decisive event itself.

■ Vestiges of a Widerstandnest on Utah Beach

The Allied Preparations

■ Amphibious «DD» tank

■ Operation P.L.U.T.O. (Pipe Line Under The Ocean)

From the spring of 1943 onwards, the COSSAC (Chief of Staff to the Supreme Allied Commander) general staff run by General Morgan, got down to the business of preparing the invasion on the coast of north-western France.

As a result of their tragic experience in Dieppe, the Allies renounced launching a frontal attack on a port and chose to land directly on the beaches. However, as they needed facilities for the landing of the considerable quantities of men, vehicles and supplies required for the success of the operation, they rallied to the audacious idea launched by Winston Churchill himself. This involved building, in England, the various elements of two artificial harbours, which were to cross the Channel behind the invasion fleet in order to be assembled on site. In parallel, General Percy Hobart and his teams of engineers were working on the development of a series of special machines. Among them, the famous DD (Duplex Drive) amphibious tanks, designed to be launched at sea and to head for the shore under their own steam, in order to give the artillery support to the first waves of assault that their predecessors had so cruelly lacked at Dieppe.

Others were designed to clear the beaches of the different obstacles with which they were covered, opening breaches in mine-fields and enabling the troops to rapidly cross walls and anti-tank trenches. As for the special services, they were busy misleading the Germans as to the Allies' intentions: within the framework of the «Fortitude» misinformation operation they multiplied the clues hinting at an attack in the Pas-de-Calais.

With support from war bonds, British, American and Canadian factories strove day and night to furnish the gigantic arsenal of the Allied armies with guns, tanks, lorries, landing barges etc. Finally, as part of operation «Bolero», hundreds of thousands of American soldiers arrived in England during the first months of 1944.

With spring came the massive aerial bombardment of the Atlantic Wall, radar stations, road and rail bridges, railway stations and air-fields. D-Day was approaching!

Its precise date depended on a whole series of parameters. First, it had to be on a full moon night in order to facilitate the task of the paratroop units that were to make drops at either extremity of the

■ Tribute to operation P.L.U.T.O.:
The «Essor» monument in Port-en-Bessin

■ American propaganda poster promoting the sale of war bonds

landing sector. The amphibious assault itself would have to be made at dawn, at mid-rising tide in order to avoid the obstacles installed on the beaches by Rommel.

The day finally settled on was the 5th of June, with the possibility of postponing until the next day or the day after. The tempest that blew up unexpectedly in the Channel forced Eisenhower to delay the departure when troops were already on board their ships.

However, trusting in the information from the meteorological services forecasting a slight improvement over the following few hours, he decided to launch the operation on the 6th of June. Conditions were still far from ideal, as there was, notably, a heavy swell, but a further postponement would have delayed the invasion for several weeks, and run the risk of depriving the Allied projects of their impetus and the indispensable element of surprise.

■ Southampton, early June. Canadian troops awaiting their departure for France

The Landing

The events on the 6th of June began unfolding shortly after midnight, when the British paratroopers dropped between the Orne and the Dives. Then it was the Americans' turn to parachute into the Cotentin peninsula. Meanwhile, a thousand RAF heavy bombers bombarded the ten heavy artillery batteries in the Seine Bay considered to be the most dangerous. At daybreak, the 8th US Air Force took over, followed by the tactical aviation.

At dawn, the disbelieving Germans discovered a sea covered with thousands of ships. Lulled into a false sense of security by the bad weather - a priori unsuitable for an invasion - and blinded by the destruction of their radar systems over the preceding weeks, they had not seen the immense Allied armada as it approached. Now it was too late to react. At 0545 hours, the warships opened fierce fire on the coastal defences.

At 0630 hours, the first American assault waves hit the beaches at Utah and Omaha. In the British and Canadian sectors, off Gold, Juno and Sword, the attack was launched an hour later, to compensate for the differences in tide times along the coast.

With the exception of Omaha, where the outcome of the battle hung in the balance for several hours, the Atlantic Wall was mercilessly rent asunder everywhere, and the Allies penetrated inland, under the protection of the air forces, omnipresent in the skies. On the beaches, the reinforcement units were coming in at a high rate.

■ **0545 hours: the American battleship USS Arkansas opening fire**

■ The first assault wave approaching Omaha Beach

■ British armoured troops landing at Ver-sur-Mer

■ Canadian propaganda poster

was a victim of contradictory orders, acted but to no great effect. During the evening and night of the 6th to the 7th of June, in order to slow the arrival of enemy reinforcements, the Allied aviation systematically reduced ten Lower Normandy towns to rubble, causing the death of 3,000 civilians. By the evening of the 6th of June, the Allies had landed over 155,000 soldiers and 20,000 vehicles. Their losses (killed, wounded and disappeared) numbered around 10,000 men; slightly fewer than had been predicted. With the exception of Omaha, where the Americans were still fighting with their backs to the sea, the bridgeheads had been developed six miles or so inland. Nevertheless, not all of D-Day's objectives had been achieved. Although Bayeux was liberated the next day, Caen was another matter: the British and Canadians were not to capture the town until the 9th of July, a whole month after the estimated date.

Whereas the invasion succeeded with relatively little fighting, the liberation of Normandy was to take much longer and be much more trying than was at first imagined. The Germans regrouped and put up fierce resistance everywhere. The Allies were to be thwarted for many long weeks both around Caen, which was protected by the formidable steel rampart of the Panzer divisions, and in the Cotentin, where the Americans were to become bogged down in the exhausting «battle of the hedgerows». It was not until the end of July that the decisive breakthrough, resulting from operation Cobra, was finally achieved to the west of Saint-Lô. One month later, the debris of the German armies that managed to escape from the Falaise pocket, where they had allowed themselves to become trapped, crossed the Seine and quit the major part of the French territory without further ado.

For the time being, the Germans were unable to check the offensive. They were bogged down due to the dithering of their high command and the destruction of a part of their means of communication through sabotage by the Resistance. The only armoured division near the coast, the 21st Panzer, which

LES ARMEES ALLIEES DEBARQUENT

82nd DIV. PARAS U.S

101st DIV. PARAS U

Portland

Torquay

4th DIV. US

Fowey

29th DIV. US

Plymouth

Falmouth

Anti-submarine patrols

M a n c h e

JER

14

🜨 **343**

🜨 **353**

🜨 **266**

Saint-Br

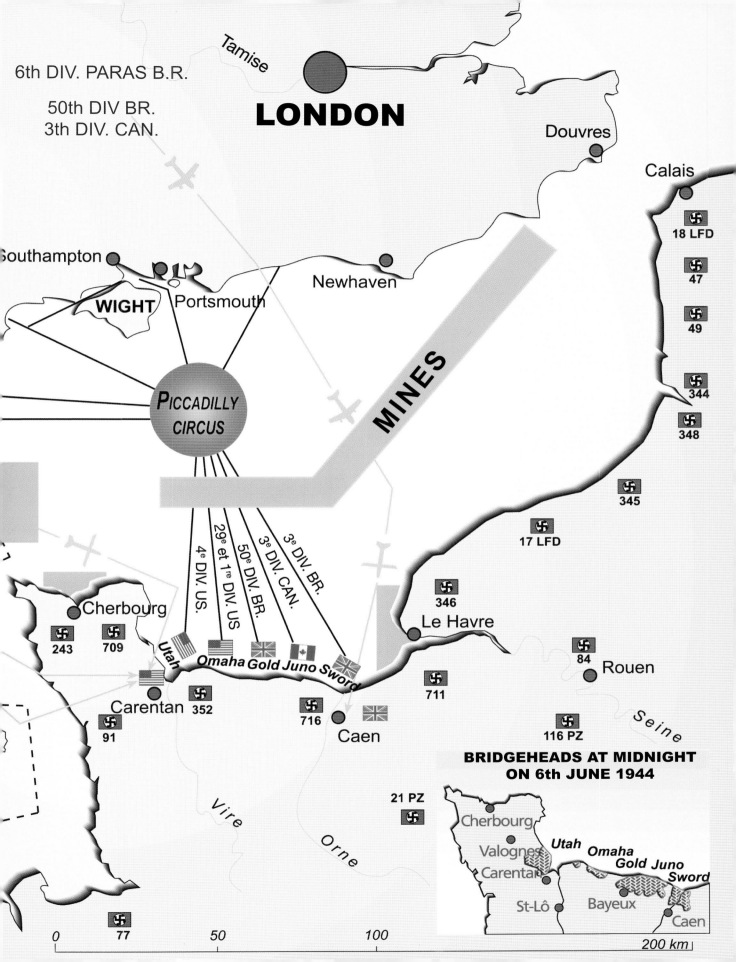

6th DIV. PARAS B.R.

50th DIV BR.
3th DIV. CAN.

Tamise

LONDON

Douvres

Calais

⊕ 18 LFD

⊕ 47

⊕ 49

⊕ 344

⊕ 348

Southampton

WIGHT

Portsmouth

Newhaven

MINES

⊕ 345

⊕ 17 LFD

PICCADILLY CIRCUS

⊕ 346

Le Havre

⊕ 84 Rouen

Cherbourg

⊕ 243   ⊕ 709

Utah

4e DIV. US.

29e et 1re DIV. US

50e DIV. BR.

3e DIV. CAN.

3e DIV. BR.

Omaha Gold Juno Sword

⊕ 711

Carentan   ⊕ 352

⊕ 716

Caen

⊕ 91

Seine

⊕ 116 PZ

BRIDGEHEADS AT MIDNIGHT
ON 6th JUNE 1944

Vire

Orne

21 PZ
⊕

⊕ 77

0   50   100   200 km

Cherbourg

Valognes

Carentan

Utah

Omaha

Gold Juno

Sword

St-Lô

Bayeux

Caen

■ Utah beach in June 1944

Utah Beach

The Plain region, on the east coast of the Cotentin peninsula between Montebourg and Carentan, is an area of low-lying, humid countryside; a landscape consisting of hedgerows and marshes that become flooded every winter. Ever since the 17th Century, it has been predominantly given over to dairy farming. The wide sandy beaches that stretch along the coast rise up to a line of dunes that separate them from the marshes that are crossed by means of raised «causeways».

■ 4th Invantry
Division Insignia

■ 82nd Airborne Division
Insignia

■ 101st Airborne
Division Insignia

Marshall Rommel, well aware that this sector of the coast lent itself ideally to an amphibious attack, increased visits to the site to reinforce the defensive system. As a result, the dunes from the Baie des Veys to Saint-Vaast-la-Hougue were studded with a good thirty or so «resistance nests», or «Widerstandnesten» (WN). Heavy batteries were installed on the higher ground inland, notably in Azeville, Saint-Marcouf, Morsalines, la Pernelle, etc. Finally, in order to counter the risk of an attack by paratroopers, the Germans caused the valleys of the Douves and the Merderet to become flooded, transforming a good part of the surrounding countryside into marshland.

■ Paratroopers from the 101st Airborne Division

In their initial plans, the Allies had not intended to land on the Cotentin coast. It was not before December 1943 that Eisenhower and Montgomery decided to add a supplementary beach, west of the Baie des Veys, to those already selected on the Calvados coast, so as to be able to capture the port of Cherbourg more rapidly. The place chosen, code-named Utah Beach (after one of the American states), stretched from Sainte-Marie-du-Mont to Quinéville, and included a roughly 1-mile wide assault zone down from the Vareville dunes. The task of leading the attack had been entrusted to General Barton's 4th Invantry Division.

The general staff decided to drop two parachute divisions here during the night before the invasion in order to protect this sector. Their mission was to check the German counter-offensives against the beaches. General Ridgway's 82nd Airborne was to capture the important crossroads at Saint-Mère-Eglise and the bridges over the Merderet. The 101st Airborne, under General Taylor, was to deploy its efforts to take control of the access routes behind Utah Beach. Between midnight and 3am, nearly a thousand C-47 Dakota transport planes dropped over 13,000 paratroopers over the Cotentin peninsula, the vanguard of the Allied armies on French soil. However, for the most part, the drop was undertaken in difficult conditions. Many aircraft, targeted by the FLAK, were in a hurry to get away from danger and, consequently, were flying too high and too fast. The paratroopers often landed a long way from the drop zone they had been assigned, sometimes dozens of miles away from the planned site. Many became lost, entangled in trees or stuck in the marshes; some even drowned there, with the result that many units were incapable of regrouping to carry out their missions. Fortunately, this dispersion threw the Germans, who were unable to calculate the enemy's strength and position. The result was a night of fighting in the Norman countryside that was as sporadic as it was confused.

In the morning, the paratroopers took hours to regroup and to make a first contact, near Pouppeville, with the leading units of the 4th Division, which had landed at dawn before la Madeleine, the beach at Saint-Marie-du-Mont. The following days were consecrated to cleaning up pockets of German resistance inside the American lines and to the extension of the bridgehead. Further south, the capture of Carentan, on the 12th of June, made it possible to link up with the troops en route from Omaha Beach. To the north, the capture of the Azeville and Crisbecq batteries were the major steps on the road to Cherbourg.

■ The GI's set foot on Utah Beach

SAINTE-MÈRE-ÉGLISE
1. Church (stained glass windows – John Steele mannequin)
2. Landing Committee signal monument (square)
3. Stele - Alexandre Renaud (square)
4. Commemorative plaque in memory of paratroopers killed on the 6th of June, rue de la Cayenne
5. Freedom Milestone, Kilometre «O» (town hall)
6. Plaque - «First town liberated» (town hall)
7. Stele - civilian victims (town hall)
8. Stele - Generals Ridgway and Gavin (town hall)
9. Stele - 505th Parachute Regiment (south town entrance)
10. Stele marking the provisional cemetery N°1 (road to Chef-du-Pont)
11. Stele marking the provisional cemetery N°2 (sports ground)

LA FIÈRE
12. Paratroopers Memorial Monument (Iron Mike)

AMFREVILLE-CAUQUGNY
13. 507th Regiment (82nd Airborne Division) Memorial
14. Stelae - "Timmes orchard"
15. Plaque - 507th Regiment, 82nd Airborne Division (church)

LA LONDE
16. Stele - aerodrome A6

NEUVILLE-AU-PLAN
17. Plaque – 82nd Airborne Division (opposite the church)

FRESVILLE
18. Monument in memory of lost troops from the 82nd Airborne Division

CHEF-DU-PONT
19. Stele - 508th Parachute Regiment

20. Garden of Remembrance – 508th Parachute Regiment

BRUCHEVILLE
21. Stele – aerodrome A-16 (36th Fighter Squadron)

BLOSVILLE
22. Stele marking the provisional cemetery N°3

HIESVILLE
23. Stele - General Don Pratt
24. Monument - first 101st Airborne Division hospital (castle)

ANGOVILLE-AU-PLAIN
25. Monument – 101st Airborne division nurses (church)
26. Paratroopers' stained glass window (church)

SAINTE-MARIE-DU-MONT-BOURG
27. Narrative plaques - Gilles Perrault
28. Plaque – 101st Airborne Division (town hall)
29. Monument to the Danish seamen

LA MADELEINE BEACH
30. Monument to the 4th Division
31. Stele – 90th Division
32. Federal monument commemorating the 40th anniversary of the Landings
33. Monument to the 1st Engineer Special Brigade
34. General Caffey's tomb (former bunker)
35. Freedom Milestone, kilometre «OO»
36. Stele - US Naval Reserves
37. Plaque - US Coastguards
38. Plaque commemorating the 40th anniversary of the Landings

39. Stele – French Free Air Force
40. French Free Forces stained glass window
41. US Navy plaque ("Roosevelt" cafe)

AZEVILLE
42. Stele - Aerodrome A7 (365th Fighter Squadron)

CRISBECQ
43. Stele - Aerodrome A7 (367th Fighter Squadron)

QUINEVILLE
44. Stele – 39th Regiment. 90th Division
45. Panel depicting the December 1943 raid

BEUZEVILLE-AU-PLAIN
46. Monument in memory of the 17 paratroopers killed in the crash of their C-47

FOUCARVILLE
47. Monument to the former German POW camp
48. Monument to General Leclerc's 2nd Armoured Division

BREVANDS
49. Liberation stained glass window (church)

SAINT-CÔME-DU-MONT
50. Plaque - 101st Airborne Division (museum)

CARENTAN
51. Landing Committee signal monument
52. Stele - 101st Airborne Division
53. 101st Airborne Division stained glass window (Notre-Dame church)

■ Sainte-Mère-Église and its legendary mannequin representing the paratrooper John Steele.

Sainte-Mère-Église

The church square is obviously the village's main tourist attraction. A mannequin representing the legendary John Steele, whose parachute unluckily caught on the balusters, hangs from the belfry. Inside the building there are stained glass windows where profane, military imagery meets the sacred: one represents the archangel Saint Michael (patron saint of paratroopers) killing the nazi dragon; the other depicts the virgin Mary surrounded by a host of paratroopers. Near the apse, in the shade of the trees on the square, the venerable old hand pump that was used to fight the fire on the night of the 6th of June has been piously preserved.

Not far from there is the Airborne Troops' Museum, in the garden of the house that was ravaged by flames that night

■ The Liberation stained glass window

This little Norman village owes its current international renown first of all to its mayor in 1944, Alexandre Renaud who, through his writing and initiatives, was the public relations specialist lacking in many other villages where similar events happened during the night of the 5th to the 6th of June.

The village of course also owes its fame to Daryl Zanuck's famous film «The Longest Day». We particularly remember the tragic scene showing the first paratroopers landing just after 1am right in the heart of the village. They belonged to the 101st Airborne Division and had been dropped there by mistake. Unluckily for them, part of the population, which had been roused by the alarm bell, was busy fighting a fire that had flared up shortly beforehand. The German patrol supervising the operation reacted swiftly.

A few Americans were killed, and some others managed to escape as best they could. More waves of paratroopers, belonging to the 505th Regiment of the 82nd Airborne Division, were to follow and receive an even more terrible welcome, as the whole garrison had by then been readied. Several perished before they even touched the ground.

In Sainte-Mère-Église everything is nowadays organised around the memory of the landings and of the events of the night of the 5th to the 6th of June. When strolling through the village, the visitor is likely to stumble upon Rue du General Gavin, the Hotel du 6 Juin, the Le Dakota restaurant, Rue Eisenhower, the John Steele Hotel...

The different commemorative monuments grouped in front of the town hall merit some explanation.

On either side of the milestone marking kilometre «0» on the Road to Freedom, two plaques (in French and in English) affirm that Sainte-Mère-Église was the first town on the western front to be liberated by the Allies, which, without wishing to rumple local self-esteem, is manifestly incorrect, since the 3rd Battalion of Lieutenant-Colonel Edward Krause's 505th Parachute Regiment only took control of the area at around 4.30am, whereas Ranville, in Calvados, had fallen to the British two hours earlier.

Be that as it may, the American flag hoist for the occasion is now conserved in the town hall. Less contentious, alas, is the plaque in memory of civilian victims, bearing the names of the locals killed during the Liberation, notably by the German artillery fire during the morning and afternoon of the 6th of June.

Fighting continued around the little town, which was threatened by the counter-offensives of both factions. The plaque on one of the houses in Rue de la Cayenne honouring the memory of four paratroopers killed by a shell on the 6th of June at around 5pm bears witness to the fact. Close to the town, two stelae indicate the location of the cemeteries (a third is situated in Blosville) where the bodies of 14,000 GI's killed in Normandy were provisionally buried, before being repatriated to the United States or transferred to Colleville-sur-Mer.

■ Milestone «0»
Milestone «0», inaugurated in September 1947, symbolically marks the start of the Road to Freedom that the American armies drove through France in 1944. Freedom milestones line both the branch that leads to Cherbourg, and the main route that runs through Avranches, Chartres, Fontainebleau, Reims, Verdun, etc. and continues 1,142km (713 miles) to Bastogne in Belgium.

■ Paratroopers attempting to dislodge a sniper in the belfry in Sainte-Mère-Église

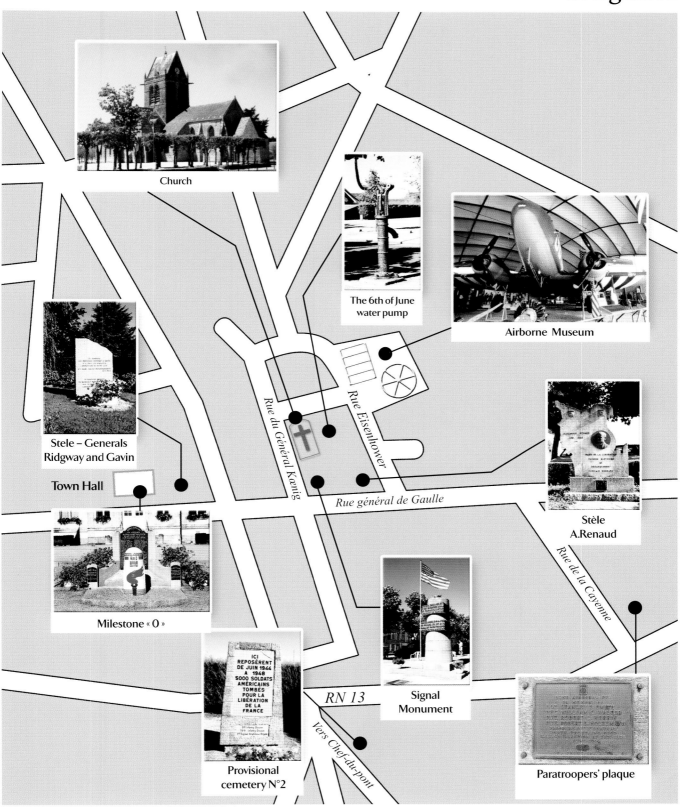

Church

The 6th of June
water pump

Airborne Museum

Stèle – Generals
Ridgway and Gavin

Town Hall

Stèle
A.Renaud

Rue du Général Kœnig

Rue Eisenhower

Rue général de Gaulle

Rue de la Cayenne

Milestone « 0 »

Signal
Monument

RN 13

Vers Chef-du-pont

Provisional
cemetery N°2

Paratroopers' plaque

La Fière Bridge

■ La Fière Bridge

From the 6th to the 9th of June the La Fière bridge and the raised causeway across the flooded valley of the Merderet were the scene of violent clashes. For the paratroopers of the 82nd Airborne Division, it was both a matter of holding the crossing to prevent the adversary from marching on Sainte-Mère-Église and getting a foothold on the opposite bank, so as to link up with their comrades who were stuck on the west side of the river, still scattered and isolated behind the enemy lines. For four days they had to hold out against murderous artillery fire and repel several attempts by grenadiers from the 9lst German Infantry Division, made with armoured support, before being able to begin their push towards Cauquigny. In 1997, a memorial paying tribute to the memory of the American airborne troops was erected on the rising slope near the La Fière bridge. The key element is «Iron Mike», an imposing statue of a determined paratrooper, a replica of the one at the infantry training college in Fort Benning in the USA. A plaque set by veterans from the 508th Regiment of the 82nd Airborne Division recalls the death of 336 of their comrades during the Battle of Normandy, and the wounding or disappearance of 825 others.

■ Iron Mike.

Chef-du-Pont

Along with La Fière, the bridge crossing the Merderet on the road out of the village of Chef-du-Pont was the only way across the river in the drop zone. Because of this, its capture was one of the priorities assigned to the men from the 508th Regiment of the 82nd Airborne Division.

As German resistance was particularly vigorous, it was not captured until the 9th of June, after heavy losses. Near the bridge, there is a stele dedicated to the combatants of the 508th Parachute Regiment and, on the other side of the road, a small garden of remembrance has been created at the instigation of the unit's veterans.

■ 508th Parachute Regiment garden of remembrance.

Amfreville

The 507th Parachute Regiment (82nd Airborne Division) were to land in Drop Zone "T", in the immediate vicinity of Amfreville. It proved to be one of the most catastrophic drops on the night of the 5th to the 6th of June. After having erred throughout the best part of the night, Lieutenant-Colonel Timmes, who was in command of the 2nd Battalion, finally managed to reassemble several dozen men and headed for Amfreville in the morning. Repelled by the Germans who maintained a steadfast hold on the village, he was forced into retreat within an orchard to the east of the village, where he and his men were to endure several days of bitter enemy fire. Amfreville was only freed on the 11th of June by a battalion from the 90th Infantry Division which had progressed from Utah Beach.

A memorial park, inaugurated in 2002, pays homage to the 507th Regiment. Visitors to the park can appreciate "The Beginning", a striking 5-metre high monument representing a paratrooper falling from the sky. Furthermore, several stelae, erected in the "Timmes orchard" remind us of the different units which fought in the sector.

■ 507th Parachute Regiment Memorial

■ Stele General Don Pratt.

A hundred or so Waco gliders carrying reinforcements, jeeps, 57mm guns, munitions and various different supplies for the paratroopers were dropped at 4am on the night of the 5th to the 6th of June. This was a first attempt and the experiment resulted in many accidents, many of the aircraft crashing into hedges. This was the fate that befell the glider carrying General Don Pratt, second-in-command of the 101st Airborne Division, who was killed outright, his neck broken. He had the sad privilege of being the first General the Allies lost in the Battle of Normandy. A stele has been set up not far from the pasture where the accident happened. Other gliders landed during the evening of the 6th of June and the morrow, in conditions that were often no less dramatic.

■ A crashed Waco glider.

La Londe

On the little road from Sainte-Mère to Beuzeville (DI7) in the hamlet of La Londe, at the edge of a field, a stele recalls the establishment here of one of the first American airfields in Normandy in 1944. Construction work on the A-6 aerodrome started on the 7th of June. The runway, which was 1,800 metres (1,962 yards) long, went into service on the 12th, and was used until the end of July by the 371st Fighter Squadron, equipped with P-47 Thunderbolts.

The whole set-up covered about 100 hectares (250 acres). The Americans built thirty such airfields in Normandy, most of which were in the Cotentin or the Bessin. They enabled squadrons of fighters and fighter-bombers to give vital support to the troops on the ground and played a crucial role in the Battle of Normandy.

■ Construction of the La Londe site.

■ La Londe stele.

The village of Sainte-Marie-du-Mont

■ Monument to the Danish seamen .

On the night of the 5th to the 6th of June 1944, a number of troops from the 101st Airborne Division landed in the vicinity of the village of Sainte-Marie-du-Mont. Some of them even landed in the very centre of the village. All night long, sporadic skirmishes and fighting took place. The village was finally cleared and liberated by paratroopers on the morning of the 6th of June. The first troops from the 4th Infantry Division, who had set foot on the La Madeleine beach at dawn, arrived in the afternoon to effect the junction. A dozen panels on the houses on the square in front of the church recount the events of that night in anecdotal form. The texts were drafted by the writer Gilles Perrault, a local citizen. Two extremely complementary museums have recently been opened on either side of the church square: the Occupation Museum and the Liberation Museum.

Along the road that leads from Sainte-Marie-du-Mont to the sea, there is a monument dedicated to the memory of the 800 Danish seamen who took part in the landings. They had set sail for Britain with their ships when the Germans invaded their country in April 1940.

■ The Sainte-Marie-du-Mont water pump, today and yesterday .

Sainte-Marie-du-Mont • La Madeleine

■ Red Beach general quarters.

Sainte-Marie-du-Mont owes its fame primarily to its beach «La Madeleine», three miles from the village, and universally known nowadays by its code-name Utah Beach. The 8th Regiment of General Barton's 4th Division landed there at 0630 hours, with support from amphibious tanks. It landed about a mile and a half south of the intended place. This proved to be a providential error, as the German defences were considerably weaker there. The barges were swept down the coast to their port side by the coastal currents and landed opposite WN 5, which had been severely damaged by the preliminary bombardments, and put up merely token resistance. The beach was rapidly cleared of the obstacles littering it by the engineers, and the main body of troops was able to land unhindered, in spite of sporadic firing from the battery at Crisbecq, before heading inland to establish contact with the paratroopers. The 4th Division lost (killed, wounded and disappeared) no more than 200 men on the 6th of June. Between D-Day and the end of the month of October 1944, 836,000 men 220,000 vehicles and 725,000 tonnes of supplies were landed on the beaches between Sainte-Marie-du-Mont and Saint-Martin-de Varreville.

Around the Utah Beach Museum, a large number of monuments have been erected in tribute to the various units that took part in the landings, particularly the 4th and 90th Divisions. On the occasion of the 40th anniversary of the invasion, the American government had an 8-metre-high column of granite erected here. It bears the ins-cription, «The United States in a homage of pro-found gratitude to its sons who gave their lives for the liberation of these beaches on 6th June 1944». The memorial to the 1st Engineer Special Brigade, the oldest edifice on the site, was inaugurated in June 1945 by Colonel Caffey, the unit's former commander. It stands over one of the former WN 5 blockhouses, which now houses a memorial crypt. This same Colonel Caffey was the instigator of the sixty-odd special signposts that are dedicated to the memory of those of his men who died in com-bat, and whose names have been given to various roads around Utah Beach.

Sainte-Marie-du-Mont • La Madeleine at a glance

Monument to the
1st Engineer Special Brigade

Milestone "OO"

90th US Invantry
Division Stele

Monument to the
4th US Division

Monumented erected by the
American government in 1984

Sainte-Marie-du-Mont

■ Monument to the 1st Engineer Special Brigade, inaugurated in June 1945.

■ The visitor who has already seen Milestone «0» at Sainte-Mère-Eglise, marking the start of the Road to Freedom, may be surprised to discover Milestone «00» at Utah Beach. The municipal council of Sainte-Marie-du-Mont, considering that the liberation of France had in fact started on La Madeleine beach and not at Sainte-Mère-Eglise, decided to erect a second milestone, also inaugurated in September 1947.

■ One of General Caffey's signposts.

■ Monument to the 1st Engineer Special Brigade, erected on a WN5 bunker.

■ Canon de 50mm.

■ The bunkers of the Crisbecq battery measured 14 metres x 14 metres, and 7 metres high (46 x 46 x 23 feet). They were covered with a slab of concrete 3.5 metres (nearly 12 feet) thick.

A CLOSER LOOK at the CRISBECQ-SAINT-MARCOUF BATTERY

Left to the elements for sixty years and, consequently, difficult to access, the Crisbecq battery has been renovated since 2004 upon the initiative of the enthusiast, Philippe Tanne.

Considerable work has enabled the casemates to be cleared of foliage and a number of concrete structures to be unearthed from the mud and sludge.

The installation of display cases with mannequins and period museum pieces within the underground stores and shelters helps visitors to grasp, not only the structural aspects of an element of the Atlantic Wall, but also the day-to-day life of its garrison. A genuine open-air museum well worth a visit.

■ The imposing command and firing post has two levels and an observation turret. However, the day before the Landings, it had not yet received all of its measurement equipment.

Apart from the fortresses in Le Havre and Cherbourg, the marine battery in Crisbecq, situated in a dominating position 3 km (2 miles) from the sea, was the most powerful in the whole of the Baie de Seine. It was the cornerstone of the German defences in the sector. Developed as from 1941 for the German Army, it was first of all equipped with five 155mm artillery pieces, placed within open-air vats. By the end of 1943, the battery was assigned to the Navy and was endowed with modern 210mm guns.

■ The guns in the Crisbecq battery were Czech in origin (Skoda). They could fire projectiles 210mm in diameter weighing 135 kilos (300 lbs) as far as 25 km (15 miles). Their firing rate was approxiamtely 60 rounds per hour.

The first two were situated under colossal concrete pillboxes and the third, whose bunker was still under construction in 1944, was ready for use, but uncovered. The battery had a garrison crew of 400 men and was a veritable entrenchment, complete with anti-aircraft guns and surrounded by a solid defensive perimeter consisting of machine guns, mortars and anti-tank weapons.

Because of the threat it posed to the Utah Beach landing sector, the Crisbecq battery, along with Pointe du Hoc, had been the most heavily bombarded since the beginning of the spring of 1944. During the night of the 5th to the 6th of June, another 600 tonnes of bombs fell on it.

The adjoining installations were damaged, but the artillery pieces were still intact, and able to open fire on the Allied fleet the following morning, although they did not succeed in inflicting much damage.

At 8am the first artillery post under casemate had been reduced to silence. The second was to follow an hour later, after a hit by the Battleship Nevada. However, the third, pivoting within its vat, was pointed in the direction of Utah Beach and opened fire on the landing troops, presaging genuine danger.

On the morning of the 7th of June, the men from the 22nd Regiment of the 4th US Division attacked the position, but were forced back with heavy losses. The assault was launched again the next day with massive artillery support. The Americans penetrated inside the position and began hand-to-hand fighting with the defenders, but the supporting fire on Crisbecq from the neighbouring battery at Azeville, accompanied by the garrison's vigorous counter-offensive, halted the offensive in its tracks. A renewed attempt on the 9th of June also ended in failure. The Americans abandoned their objective temporarily and pursued their advance on Quinéville and Montebourg. Crisbecq was isolated and surrounded but it still held on, in spite of severe losses in the garrison. On the 11th of June, the battery commander, *Oberleutnant zur See* (sub-lieutenant or ensign) Ohmsen, received the order to evacuate. During the night he successfully led the 78 of his men that were still fit through the American lines to the German positions, even though they were 12km (7 miles) away. On the 12th of June, the Americans captured the Crisbecq battery without a fight to find a mere 20 severely wounded soldiers that had been left behind.

■ The infirmery was located within an R-621 type shelter.

■ Inside a personnel shelter.

Leaving the coast road, the visitor will discover the Azeville battery a few miles inland on slightly higher ground. It consisted of four 105mm Schneider guns concealed in bunkers (camouflaged to resemble houses) that were set in pairs on each side of the road, and completed by munition stores and shelters for the personnel. Because of the insufficient range of these guns (6 miles), the Azeville battery was unable to intervene usefully against the landings on Utah Beach.

On the other hand, its garrison put up vigorous resistance against the men from the 4th US Division which tried to capture it as of the 7th of June. The garrison, nevertheless, finished by surren-

■ In 1944, this bunker was camouflaged to resemble a dwelling house.

dering on the 9th of June under attack from flamethrowers. As well as the bunkers, it is now possible to visit the rather unique system comprising 350 metres of subterranean corridors linking the different parts of the battery and to view a film on the construction of the Atlantic Wall.

Quinéville

The Americans captured Quinéville on the evening of the 14th of June. Many fortifications are still visible on the beach at the northernmost point of Utah Beach, notably a former bunker that has been converted into a café, and an anti-tank wall.

A battery housing four 105mm guns was situated on Mont Coquerel, the hill behind the town. Before the Mémorial de la Liberté retrouvée (Refound Liberty Memorial), a panel explains the nocturnal reconnaissance mission accomplished by a Franco-British commando unit in December 1943 that was part of the preparations for the landings.

■ Former Quinéville bunker converted into a cafe.

■ The Americans entering Carentan

Carentan

On the 9th of June, the 101st Airborne Division launched an offensive in the direction of Carentan, whose capture would enable them to link up with the troops coming from Omaha, who had just captured Isigny. Attacking from Saint-Côme-du-Mont (where one can visit the Dead Man's Corner Museum), the paratroopers had no choice but to take the main Route Nationale 13, the only way through the flooded marshes around the river Douve. The «Battle of the Carentan Causeway» lasted three days and was characterised by the bitter struggle to capture four bridges solidly defended by the Germans. The final assault was launched on 11th June from a small plot of ground whose location is today indicated by a stele. The next day, the Americans entered the town which had been partially destroyed by bombs and shelling.

Saint-Martin-de-Varreville

■ General Leclerc.

The road that runs along the coast from Sainte-Marie-du-Mont to Quinéville, which is referred to as "the Allies' Road",
is littered with very numerous vestiges of the Atlantic Wall, in particular before the village of Ravenoville. In Saint-Martin-de-Varreville, at the spot initially intended for the assault on the 6th of June, a monument indicates the landing, on the 1st of August 1944, of General Leclerc's 2nd Armoured Division, the first major French unit to join the Battle of Normandy and the liberation of France.

■ Monument to the 2nd Armoured Division.

The arrival of the first wave of assault

Omaha Beach

The Bessin consists of pastureland and has a long history of dairy farming. The famous «Isigny butter» has made a major contribution to the region's reputation.

From the rocks at Grandcamp as far as Arromanches, the coast is for the most part lined by steep limestone cliffs, rising several dozen metres above the sea.

The coast subsides seaward from the villages of Vierville, Saint-Laurent and Colleville to form a gap a little less than four miles long consisting of a mound that slopes fairly steeply down to the beach to which access is gained by small, high-sided valleys.

■ The Gi's seek refuge behind the beach obstacles.

The site, by reason of its topography, was easy to defend. There were no less than fourteen *Widerstandnesten*, for the most part implanted at the entry to the valleys that were barred by anti-tank walls and pillboxes equipped with guns. The Germans had covered the terrain with machine gun nests, mortars, minefields and barbed wire, so the place was neither an ideal spot for landing operations nor devoid of risks, but it was the only one possible between the British sector to the east at Arromanches, and Utah, the second American beach on the Cotentin coast.

In March 1944, the beach was code-named Omaha (after the town in the state of Nebraska). Three months later, it entered the history books with the nickname «Bloody Omaha», because of the terrible losses sustained there by the 1st and 29th US Divisions of General Gerow's 5th Corps.

■ Men from the Engineers tend to victims of a wrecked landing barge.

The first waves of infantry, which landed at 0630 hours, were welcomed by sustained machine gun, mortar and gun fire and were pinned down on the beach. The night's aerial bombardments and the naval artillery barrage just before the offensive had made very little impact on the German defences, which were largely intact and set about strafing the beach, strewing death in the ranks of

■ Landing of the Military Police

the assailants. The terrible scenes at the beginning of Steven Spielberg's film «Saving Private Ryan» (1998) are without doubt very close to reality. To confound their bad luck, nearly all of the amphibious tanks sank before they reached the coast, thus depriving the infantry of precious artillery support. For hours the situation worsened. The beach, which was becoming ever smaller as the tide rose, was cluttered with cadavers rolling around in the waves, countless wounded men and the smoking carcasses of machines destroyed by shells. The barges bringing reinforcements became impaled on or were blown up by the obstacles that the engineers, whose units had been decimated, had not had time to remove.

After an ordeal that lasted several hours for the American soldiers, the situation at last began to turn to their advantage. As they could not make it up the valleys, which were too well defended, the GI's managed to scale the escarpment, proof of their energetic bravery, at the end of the morning, and to pen-etrate onto the plateau in small groups, whence they could attack the enemy, whose resistance was weakening, from the rear.

On the evening of D-Day, the Omaha bridgehead was little over a mile deep, yet the Americans had achieved the most important thing. The operation, which had got off to an appalling start, was nevertheless successfully completed, but at what a price! Over 3,000 men had been lost (fifteen times more than at Utah Beach), including – officially – one thousand dead. The 5th Corps, which had been given such a rough ride on the 6th of June, rectified the situation in spectacular fashion over the next few days, making the most of the collapse of German resistance in the sector. The 29th Division broke through to the west, liberating Isigny on the 9th of June and advancing rapidly in the direction of Saint-Lô and Carentan, thus joining up three days later with the Utah Beach sector. On its left, the 1st Division drove straight ahead into the Bessin, reaching Caumont-l'Éventé, twenty miles or so inland, on the 13th of June.

On site at Omaha, the very large number of monuments and stelae to be found along the remains of the Atlantic Wall, recall the awful sacrifice of the various units engaged in battle on the 6th of June 1944. There are three museums to be visited at Vierville, Saint-Laurent and Colleville, not forgetting the recent and remarkable Visitor Center built by the United States government within the American military cemetery, inaugurated on the 6th of June 2007.

■ After fierce combat on the morning of the 6th of June, the American troops landed en masse on Omaha Beach.

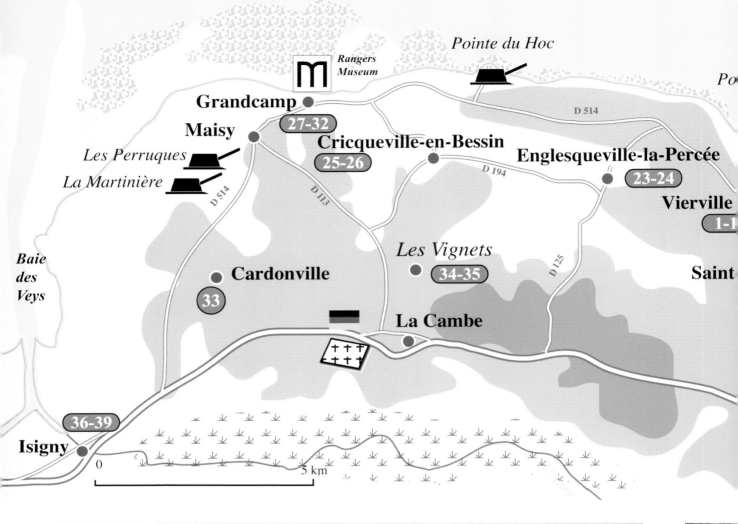

Pointe du Hoc

Rangers Museum

Grandcamp

27-32

Maisy

Les Perruques

La Martinière

D 514

Cricqueville-en-Bessin

25-26

D 113

D 194

Englesqueville-la-Percée

23-24

Vierville

1-1

Les Vignets

34-35

D 125

Cardonville

33

La Cambe

Baie des Veys

✝ ✝ ✝

Saint

36-39

Isigny

0   5 km

Po

■ A rhino barge, loaded with men and supplies, providing a shuttle service between ships and the shore

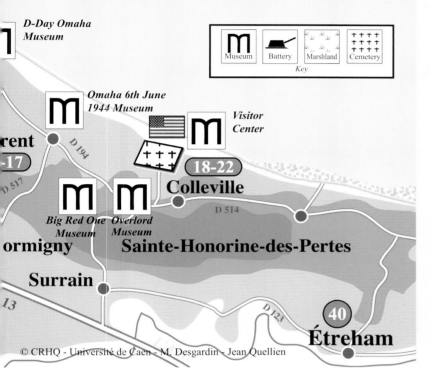

Manche

e la Percée

D-Day Omaha Museum

Omaha 6th June 1944 Museum

Visitor Center

M	⌐	⁂	✝✝✝✝
Museum	Battery	Marshland	Cemetery

Key

Colleville

18-22

rent

-17

D 517

D 194

D 514

Big Red One Museum

Overlord Museum

ormigny

Sainte-Honorine-des-Pertes

Surrain

13

D 123

40

Étreham

© CRHQ - Université de Caen - M. Desgardin - Jean Quellien

VIERVILLE
1. Monument to the National Guard
2. Milestone of the 58th Artillery Battalion
3. Plaque - 29th Engineers Division
4. Stele - 6th Engineer Special Brigade
5. Stele - 29th Division
6. Stele – resistance fighter Jean Sainteny
7. Plaque – 5th Rangers Battalion
8. Elements of the floating causeway of the artificial harbour
9. Plaque – 81st Mortar Battalion and 110th Artillery Battalion (church wall)
10. Plaque – general quarters of the 11th Port (castle)
11. Stele marking the location of the provisional cemetery

SAINT-LAURENT
12. Landing Committee signal monument
13. Plaque – Operation Aquantint
14. Monument "Les Braves" (the brave)
15. Monument to the 2nd division
16. Stele – aerodrome A-21 C
17. 60th Anniversary stele

COLLEVILLE
18. Monument to the 5th Engineer Special Brigade
19. Monument to the 1st Division
20. The «Tank wall»
21. 60th Anniversary stele
22. 1st Division emblem made of pebbles

ENGLESQUEVILLE-LA-PERCEE
23. Monument to the 147th Engineer Regiment (castle)
24. Stele – aerodrome A-1 (366th Fighter Sqaudron)

CRICQUEVILLE-EN-BESSIN
25. Stele – aerodrome A-2 (354th Fighter Squadron)
26. Rangers and Colonel Rudder plaque (church)

GRANDCAMP-MAISY
27. Monument to the Guyenne and Tunisia Bomber Groups (port)
28. Rangers Monument (town hall)
29. Stele recalling General de Gaulle's visit on the 14th of June 1944 (town hall)
30. Frank Peregory site
31. Statue for Peace
32. Major Kieffer's tomb (cemetery)

CARDONVILLE
33. Stele - Aerodrome A-3 (368th Fighter Squadron)

LA CAMBE/LES VIGNETS
34. Stele - Aerodrome A-4 (367th Fighter Squadron)
35. 60th Anniversary stele

ISIGNY
36. Landing Committee signal monument (General de Gaulle's visit on the 14th of June 1944)
37. 29th Division stained-glass window (church)
38. Plaque – 175th Infantry Regiment (church)
39. Plaque – 747th Tank Battalion (church)

ÉTREHAM
40. Plaque - 1st Division (town hall)

■ A grounded landing Ship Tank

41

Vierville

Dog Green was the code-name of the assault zone at Vierville assigned to the 116th Regiment of the 29th US Infantry Division. supported on its right flank by the 5th Ranger Battalion. The losses sustained by these two units were the most severe in the Omaha sector. because of the murderous fire coming from the blockhouses guarding the valley leading up to the village. notably the pillbox housing an 88mm gun upon which the monument to the National Guard now stands. During the days immediately following the landings. urgency imposed the establishment of a provisional cemetery on the shelf between the beach and the foot of the embankment. Around 450 bodies were buried there. before being disinterred and transferred to the edge of the plateau. between Colleville and Saint-Laurent. The location of what was the first American Second World War cemetery in France is now marked by a monument. situated at the side of the road running along the seafront.

It has perhaps been forgotten: immediately after the invasion. the Allies undertook to construct. not one but two artificial harbours: the Arromanches harbour. in the British sector (Mulberry «B») is now world-famous: the other. in the American sector. has almost totally disap-

■ Monument to the National Guard

Before the war, the National Guard constituted one of the three branches of the American army, alongside the regular and the reserve troops. It was composed of militias recruited, trained and supported by the different States. Their mission was the maintenance of order in peacetime and to provide men in time of war. Several units were composed of men from the National Guard, including the 29th Division that landed on Omaha Beach on the 6th of June 1944.
Symbolically, the monument dedicated to the National Guard has been erected on the blockhouse formerly housing an 88mm gun (WN 72) that guarded the valley leading to the small town of Vierville and inflicted heavy losses on the assailants before being knocked out by a tank. On its three interior walls, bilingual texts recall the role of the National Guard during the two World Wars.

■ A jetty built on the remains of the artificial harbour

■ Religious service at the Vierville provisional cemetery

peared from memory. Yet Mulberry «A» was assembled off Vierville and Saint-Laurent. It had barely been completed when it was broken to pieces by the fierce storm that hit the Channel between the 19th and the 22nd of June. A few mere vestiges recall its short existence.

In spite of this fateful event, the Americans succeeded in landing impressive quantities of men, equipment and supplies (more than the British!) by beaching large transport ships with opening bows, the LSTs, or by means of large metal rafts, known as Rhino barges, and the DUCKW

amphibious trucks that provided the links between the large cargo vessels moored offshore and the beach.

The organisation and control of this intense traffic fell to the IIth US Port, whose headquarters were established in Vierville castle, as we are reminded by a plaque affixed to one of the entrance gate pillars.

■ Stele marking the location of the 1st American cemetery

43

Colleville

■ Insignia of the 1st US Division

The beach at Colleville was assigned to the 16th Regiment of the 1st Division, the famous «Big Red One», one of the most prestigious units in the American army. In spite of its experience, it was given equally rough treatment by the sustained fire unleashed by the Germans. Many men were only saved by the shelter afforded at the foot of the neighbouring cliffs. With vigour and courage a few small groups managed to make it onto the plateau up from Fox Green, thus contributing to tipping the scales of the terrible battle in the GI's favour. Among the commemorative monuments in the Colleville sector, one is particularly memorable, the impressive obelisk dedicated to the 1st Division that dominates the beach, on which are inscribed the names of the men who fell on the 6th of June and the following days. Beneath it, the monument to the 5th Engineer Brigade pays tribute to the engineer units, who were so particularly put to the test during the landing on Omaha Beach while they attempted to remove the obstacles from the beach, under withering enemy fire, in order to enable the barges carrying reinforcements to reach the shore.

Today, in a calm serenity very far removed from the turmoil of D-Day, hundreds of thousands of people come to visit the impressive cemetery at Colleville every year, and stand in contemplative remembrance before the 9,386 impeccably aligned white marble crosses. A father and son lie beside each other. In 33 other cases, it is brothers who are buried together. 307 graves bear the inscription «Known only to God». The Normandy American Cemetery is the only Second World War American cemetery in Normandy, apart from the Saint James Brittany Cemetery in the Manche département (4,410 graves). Fourteen thousand other GI's bodies were repatriated to the United States upon request from the bereaved families. The soldiers who lie in Colleville are not only those who died on the beaches on the 6th of June, but also the men killed elsewhere in Normandy, whose bodies were first of all buried in provisional cemeteries then exhumed some years after the war and transferred to the symbolic site at Omaha. The cemetery was inau-

44   ■ Monument to the 1st US Division

gurated in July 1956 and is built over a vast area stretching over 70 hectares (170 acres) granted to the United States by France. At the entrance to the central alley, opposite a large pool, there stands a limestone memorial of two loggias linked by arcades surrounding a 7-metre-high bronze statue representing the soul of American youth rising out of the waters. Behind the memorial is the garden of remembrance dedicated to the men who disappeared, lined by a long circular wall bearing the names of the 1,557 men whose bodies were never found.

■ Aerial view of the American cemetery at Colleville .

45

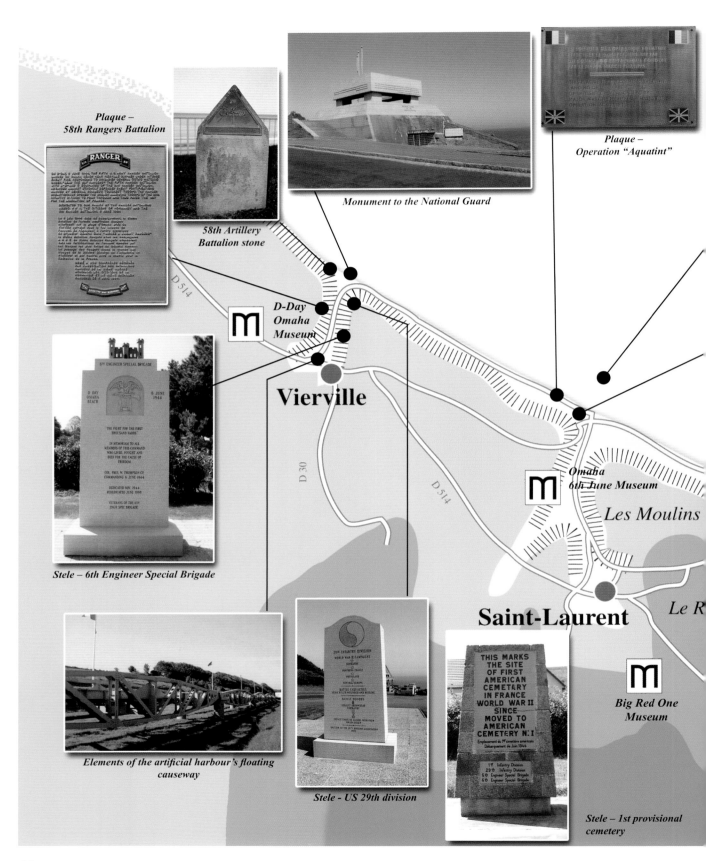

Plaque –
58th Rangers Battalion

58th Artillery
Battalion stone

Monument to the National Guard

Plaque –
Operation "Aquatint"

D-Day
Omaha
Museum

M

Vierville

Stele – 6th Engineer Special Brigade

Omaha
6th June Museum

M

Les Moulins

Saint-Laurent

Le R

M

Big Red One
Museum

Elements of the artificial harbour's floating
causeway

Stele - US 29th division

THIS MARKS
THE SITE
OF FIRST
AMERICAN
CEMETARY
IN FRANCE
WORLD WAR II
SINCE
MOVED TO
AMERICAN
CEMETERY N.1

Stele – 1st provisional
cemetery

« Les Braves » Monument

Signal Monument

US 2nd Division Monument

Monument to the 5th Engineer Special Brigade

Monument to the US 1st Division

Visitor Center

Ⓜ

Colleville-sur-Mer cemetery

P

Stele – US 1st Division

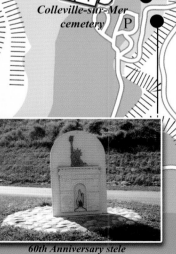

60th Anniversary stele

Colleville

"Tank wall"

D 514

Saint-Laurent-sur-Mer

A plaque affixed to the sea wall reminds passers-by that on the night of the 12th to the 13th of September 1942, Saint-Laurent was the theatre of an Allied reconnaissance raid, operation Aquatint, which ended in disaster.

A commando unit from the Small Scale Raiding Force consisting of eleven men carried by fast motorboat set out to collect information and take a few prisoners in order to interrogate them. This small group was rapidly discovered by a German patrol and engaged in a nocturnal fire-fight lasting over an hour. Three men, including the unit's commander, Major March-Phillips, perished whilst attempting to return to their motorboat, and seven others were captured. Only Captain Hayes managed to escape. He was taken in and looked after by the local Resistance, who evacuated him to Paris, but he was betrayed and fell into German hands and was subsequently executed in July 1943.

■ Vestiges of a floating element of the artificial harbour

■ Artificial harbour off Saint-Laurent and Vierville .

■ The 2nd US Division landing.

■ Monument to the 2nd US Division close to the blockhouse visible on the above photograph.

Twenty months later the men of the 116th Infantry Regiment landed on the same beach, in the sector inappropriately named «Easy», and located at the junction between the assault troops from the 1st and the 29th Divisions. However, strong coastal currents pushed their vessels eastwards, consequently jeopardising the initial plan of action. Indeed, the assailants failed to recognise any of the landmarks they had been given, hence exacerbating the general state of confusion. Opposite the «Les Moulins» hamlet, the somewhat disorientated men from the 116th Regiment (29th Division) met with ferocious resistance by the Germans that was to cost them severe losses. Here, an imposing signal monument was erected by the Landing Committee in 1959. Further east, at the entrance to the Ruquet valley, the Indian Head monument pays tribute to the 2nd Division, the first reinforcements to land on the very spot on the 7th of June.

■ "Les Braves" (the Brave) Monument
This sculpture is the work of the Parisian artist, Anilore Banon and was erected directly on the sand on Saint-Laurent beach, before the signal monument, for the 60th Anniversary of the D-Day Landings. Granted only temporary authorisation, the sculpture was due to be dismantled in 2004, in respect of coastal law. However, many defenders raised their voices in defence of its legitimacy and, a few years later... the sculpture still stands!

■ A P-38 Lightning fighter-bomber at aerodrome A-21
Whereas the fighting was still raging all around, an emergency airfield was hastily installed on the 7th of June at the edge of the plateau above Saint-Laurent beach. It was functional that same evening and was essentially used to evacuate the seriously wounded to England and fly in emergency medical equipment. Curiously named A-21, it was nevertheless the first aviation ground set up in Normandy, together with Pouppeville, to the east of Saint-Marie-du-Mont.

La Cambe

■ The German cemetery at La Cambe .

■ Overall view of the cemetery .

Very different to the cemetery at Colleville, and more romantic than conventional, the German cemetery at La Cambe is no less impressive. Over 21,200 bodies, most of them in pairs, lie in a clearing where occasional trees intersperse Maltese crosses in groups of five under little grave slabs that barely rise above the short grass.

In the centre, an imposing mound surmounted with a large cross with statues on either side, marks the place where the remains of 296 non-identified soldiers were buried.

Other German military cemeteries, designed along the same lines as La Cambe, were built in Normandy between the mid 1950s and the beginning of the 1960s in Orglandes, Marigny / La Chapelle-Enjuger (Manche), Lisieux (Calvados) and Champigny / Saint-André (Eure). They are managed by a popular association, the *Volksbund Deutsche Kriegsgräberfürsorge* (German society for the care of war graves). These cemeteries house a total of 66,000 German graves. In the Mont d'Huisne ossuary, located in the south Manche, the remains of 12,000 German soldiers, fallen in other French regions and reunited in this mausoleum upon the initiative of the *Volksbund*, lie to rest.

Englesqueville-la-Percée

On the 6th of June 1944, Colonel Rudder's Rangers mistook the Pointe de la Percée for the Pointe du Hoc, losing 40 precious minutes in attaining their objective in the process.

RANGERS

The Germans had established a large Kriegsmarine detection station called «Imme» on this promontory. It consisted of two Seeriese FuMO 214 Würzburg radar units, a Seetakt FuMO 2 long range device and a Freya FuMG 80 radar unit. The Rangers' «C» Company, which landed at the western extremity of the Omaha sector, had been given the mission of capturing the station. After having suffered heavy losses, manœuvred along the beach and climbed the cliff, they got to the station only to discover that it had been wiped out by bombs and shells.

A few rare remains in the middle of a field indicate the former location of radar station «Imme».

■ The «Freya» radar unit, destroyed by bombardments

Isigny-sur-Mer

Isigny suffered greatly from the fighting during the Liberation. In order to capture this small town, the Americans unleashed a frightful naval bombardment on the morning of the 8th of June, the aviation completing the initiative that same evening, resulting in the deaths of some thirty civilians.

During his brief visit on the 14th of June 1944, General de Gaulle delivered a speech that was both solemn and deeply emotional in the midst of the ruins of this shattered town.

■ 19th of June – civilians returning home

Grandcamp-Maisy

The Germans had established two artillery batteries behind the small fishing port of Grandcamp, intended to guard the Vire estuary at Maisy, in the hamlets of La Martinière and La Perruque. They were subjected to an aerial bombardment during the night of the 5th to the 6th of June in which the French Air Force bomber groups «Guyenne» and «Tunisie», flying four-engined Halifax bombers, took part; a monument in the port recalls their participation. Since 1944, the Perruque battery, progressively overwhelmed by thorny foliage, had somewhat fallen into oblivion. Credit is due to a British military history enthusiast, Gary Sterne, who, in 2006, uncovered the firing platforms, revealing the 155mm guns and the different struc-tures (holds and shelters) comprising this element of the Atlantic Wall. The battery was capable of reaching Utah Beach, but not Omaha, due to the insufficient range of its weapons. It was finally silenced by the Rangers on the 9th of June after a fierce battle. The site is open to visitors since 2007.

Grandcamp was liberated on the 9th of June by the American troops advancing from Omaha. General Bradley, the commander of the 1st Army, established his headquarters there. A stele in front of the town hall recalls General de Gaulle's visit on the 14th of June 1944, during his tour of the Bessin area.

A museum dedicated to the Rangers has been established on the seafront promenade, and a monument in front of the town hall also pays tribute to them. At the edge of the town, on the way to Pointe du Hoc, there is a site dedicated to the memory of Sergeant Peregory and located at the foot of a monumental statue for peace donated to the "peoples of Normandy" by the artist Yao Yuan in 2004.

■ Circular gun pit at the Maisy battery

■ Shelter

■ Monument to the French Air Forces

■ The Peregory site
On the 8th of June, the forward units of the 116th Infantry Regiment (29th US Division) were brought to a halt near Grandcamp by deadly machine gun fire.
Sergeant Peregory, heroically charged the position armed with grenades and his bayonet, capturing alone thirty-odd German soldiers. This deed won him the highest American military honour, the Congressional Medal of Honour. Frank Peregory was killed six days later near Couvains, to the north-east of Saint-Lô. His body is buried in Colleville cemetery. The monument also pays tribute to the National Guard, from which the 29th Division was recruited.

■ Bombardments on the 4th of June 1944

Pointe du Hoc

A few miles east of the small fishing port of Grandcamp, on the land around Cricqueville-en-Bessin, the vertical coastal cliff forms a promontory that overlooks a narrow shingle beach from a height of about 30 metres (100 feet): Pointe du Hoc.

The Germans had built a powerful artillery battery, capable of covering a considerable section of the coast, on this particularly favourable site.

It posed a major threat to both beaches chosen for the landing of the American troops.

The Germans, who were aware of the defensive advantages of Pointe du Hoc, built a battery there in 1942, housing six 155mm guns set in buried concrete pits open to the sky. These were guns made in France (1916 model) weighing 14 tonnes each and with a range of over 12 miles. In the spring of 1943, a firing command post was built at the very tip of the point, thus scanning a vast area. It was topped at the front by a heavy observation turret and camouflaged to resemble the structure of the cliff (the camouflaging has today disappeared) and was equipped with a powerful range finder set into a rectangular pit built into the roof of the bunker (at the foot of the present-day commemorative monument).

■ A 155mm gun in its sunken concrete emplacement

The system was completed by the many concrete shelters, most of them buried, used by the garrison or munitions stores.

The battery, which was protected by a network of barbed wire, minefields, machine-gun posts and anti-aircraft guns (FLAK) positioned at each extremity, had a crew of 200 men, 80 of whom were gunners.

At the beginning of 1944, in conformity with the instructions given by Rommel, the troops stationed here did their utmost to provide shelter for the guns to protect them from attacks from the air. By the spring, two blockhouses had been completed and a third was under construction. However, because of a lack of gun carriages, the cannons were still in their emplacements when, on the 15th of April, the Allies launched a violent bombard-ment, destroying one of them. In order to save the five others, the battery commander decided to transport them secretly inland.

■ Small storage spaces for munitions and material were set into the walls of the gun housings

■ Blockhouse

The blockhouses on Pointe du Hoc (of H 679 type) were of approximately 15 metres (50 feet) by 15 metres, the construction of each requiring 600m3 (almost 2,000 cubic feet) of concrete and 40 tonnes of metal framework. The side walls were nearly 3 metres (over 9 feet) thick and had to support a roof two metres thick. Inside, there was a firing chamber, where the gun was installed and two compartments at the back of the bunker where the munitions were stored. The opening was protected by a tiered structure aimed at neutralising as much as possible the shrapnel from enemy fire.

■ A corridor with security doors in a munitions store

■ The Rangers climbing the rock face using ladders and ropes

■ Part of the cliff collapsed under the bombardment

Pointe du Hoc
at a glance

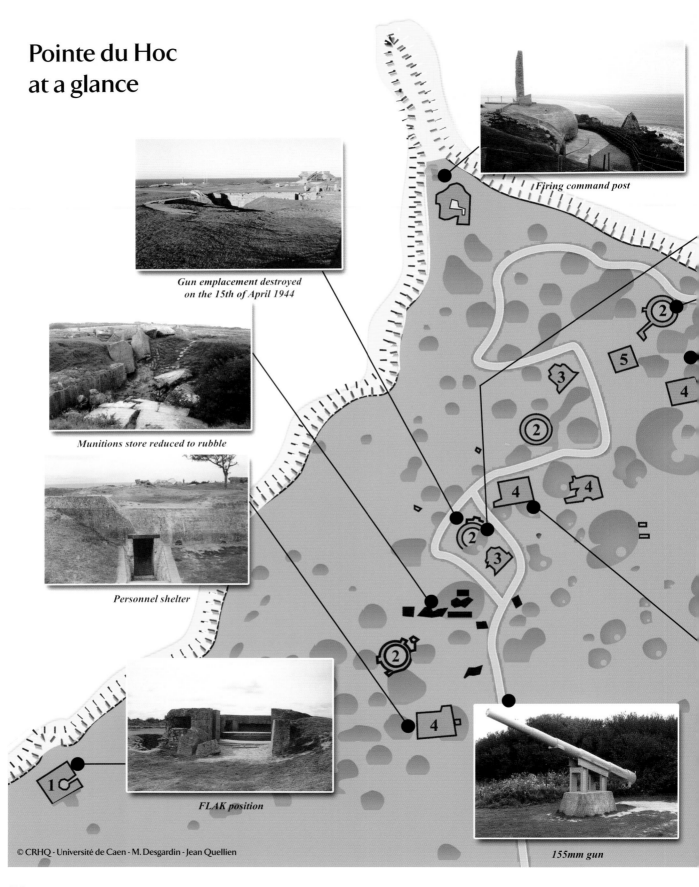

Firing command post

Gun emplacement destroyed
on the 15th of April 1944

Munitions store reduced to rubble

Personnel shelter

FLAK position

155mm gun

© CRHQ - Université de Caen - M. Desgardin - Jean Quellien

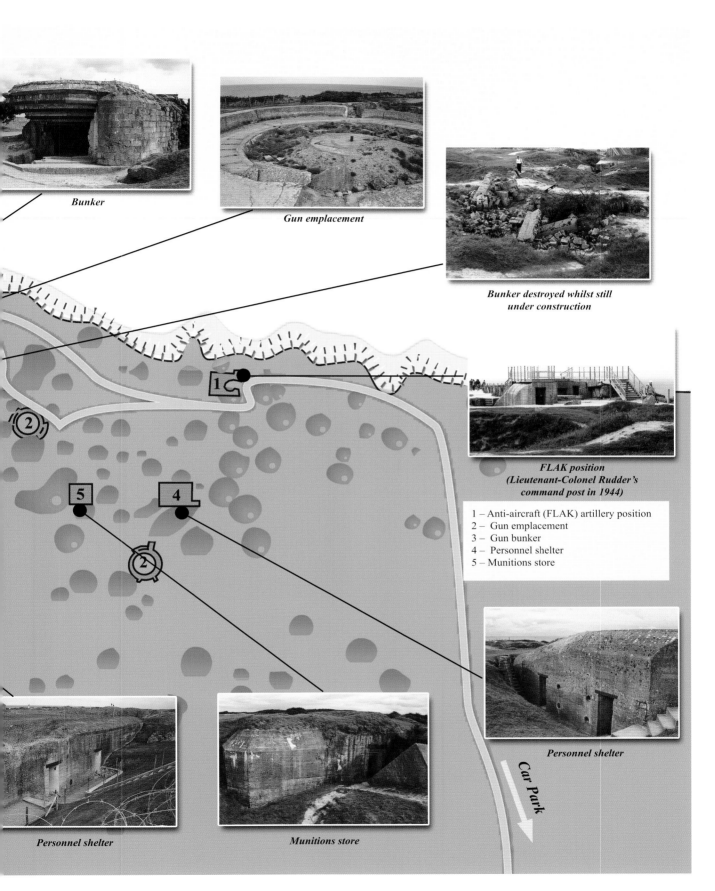

Bunker

Gun emplacement

**Bunker destroyed whilst still
under construction**

**FLAK position
(Lieutenant-Colonel Rudder's
command post in 1944)**

1 – Anti-aircraft (FLAK) artillery position
2 – Gun emplacement
3 – Gun bunker
4 – Personnel shelter
5 – Munitions store

Personnel shelter

Car Park

Personnel shelter

Munitions store

■ Lieutenant-Colonel Rudder's command post, located within a FLAK firing position, in 1944 and today

Aware of the threat that the guns on Pointe du Hoc posed to the Utah and Omaha landing beaches, Allied strategists had decided to annihilate them. In spite of the bombardments that were going to be stepped up all through May and June, it was decided, to be on the safe side, to mount an assault on the position and capture it at dawn on D-Day, by scaling the cliffs using ropes and ladders. This formidable mission was assigned to the 2nd Ranger Battalion commanded by Colonel James E. Rudder.

The men of D, E, and F Companies, who were transported to the site in barges, succeeded in achieving the incredible exploit of scaling the cliffs in a few mere minutes, in spite of the very slippery rock face, ropes sodden and heavy with sea water and the fire of the defending troops. A ferocious fight, more deadly than the climb itself, started in a lunar, crater-strewn landscape.

A considerable surprise awaited the Rangers. They discovered that large wooden beams replacing the guns had been installed in the sunken vats. The guns themselves were discovered later by a patrol about a mile south of the Pointe. They were set up in a firing configuration in a sunken lane but seemed to have been abandoned: the patrol rendered them harmless, destroying their breech blocks with explosives.

Now began terrible long hours for Rudder's men, isolated on Pointe du Hoc, deprived of reinforcements and subjected to a powerful German counter-offensives coming from all sides. They were only delivered on the 8th of June, around midday, by

■ Lieutenant-Colonel Rudder.

troops that had landed at Omaha. Of the 225 Rangers embarked upon this mad escapade, only 90 were still capable of fighting. Almost 80 of their comrades had lost their lives on this tiny corner of Norman soil. Their names are inscribed on a stele inside the firing command post. Another plaque paying them tribute has been set in the Cricqueville church.

Pointe du Hoc is today one of the most frequently visited historic sites in Normandy. If hundreds of thousands of people every year can now discover its spectacular appearance, sculpted by the explosion of bombs and shells, it is thanks to the intervention of the Grandcamp tourist information office who, in

■ The Pointe du Hoc Monument •
The monument was erected in 1960 upon the initiative of the Pointe du Hoc Committee. This large shaft of granite, which stands at the edge of the cliff on the former firing command post, symbolises the dagger the Rangers stabbed into the Germans' Atlantic Wall defences.

1945, requested that the site be conserved in the state it was in at the end of the fighting, thus avoiding the landfill and the bunker destruction that were undertaken in many other places. Later, this initiative was relayed by the Pointe du Hoc Committee, comprising local and regional figures. Since the agreement signed in 1979 with the French state, the management of these sites has been entrusted to the American Battle Monuments Commission. The worrying erosion of the cliff-face constitutes a genuine threat to the site's longevity. Visitors to Pointe du Hoc will find useful complementary information when they visit the Rangers' Museum in Grandcamp.

■ The Rangers monument at Grandcamp

■ The British 50th Infantry Division landing on Gold Beach

Gold beach Arromanches

Gold Beach is the code-name given to the coastal sector assigned to the British 30th Corps, stretching from the American Omaha Beach the Canadian Juno Beach. East of Arromanches, the cliffs give way to a low-lying coast behind which there is an area of marshland. General Graham's 50th Northumbrian Division was to spearhead the landings there, between Asnelles and Ver-sur-Mer.

This experienced unit had distinguished itself in North Africa, notably during the Battle of El-Alamein, but it had also been active in France in 1940 and lived through the miraculous evacuation of troops from the Dunkirk beaches.

For the unit, this 6th of June 1944 was something of a sweet revenge. The invasion, led by the 69th and 231st Brigades, began at 0735, an hour later than in the two American sectors, as a result of the difference in tide times.

As was his habit, General Montgomery ordered a massive bombardment of the German positions by the naval artillery, although the Air Force had already dropped tonnes of bombs on them. The enemy resistance was concentrated at the two extremities of the sector, particularly in Asnelles.

■ Men from the 50th Division progressing inland

Support from the special tanks of the 79th Division was to be needed to achieve their goal. after fighting that was very costly in men's lives. However, in the middle of the sector the mediocre unit consisting of Russians that had been drafted into the Wehrmacht was overcome without difficulty. hence facilitating the British breakthrough across the marshes, where they opened passages through the minefields using «Flail» tanks. Thenceforth. the troops, with reinforcements from the division's reserve brigade. drove inland without encountering excessive opposition. On the evening of the 6th of June. the British had landed 25.000 men and had control of a quadrilateral of about 6 miles by 6. For the most part. their objectives had been achieved. The forward units of the 50th Division had come within view of the main RN 13 roadlink and had reached the outskirts of Bayeux. On their left flank. they had linked up with the Canadians who had landed on Juno Beach. On the other hand. on their right flank. whereas Arromanches had been captured. Port-en-Bessin was still in German hands and contact with the Americans had not yet been made. as a consequence of the awful difficulties that the latter had encountered at Omaha Beach.

During the days following the invasion. the British continued their drive south before being brought up short by the arrival in the sector of a formidable German armoured division. the Panzer Lehr. From

that moment on. the front was brought to a standstill. along a line running from Caumont-l'Éventé through Tilly-sur-Seulles to Caen. until the end of June. Tilly was to be the scene of ferocious clashes.

■ The slippery ramps of the Landing Craft led to many falls. To the left a self-propelled SEXTON gun.

■ 6th June 1944 – British soldiers fraternising with the locals in Ver-sur-Mer

■ Insignia of the 50th Division

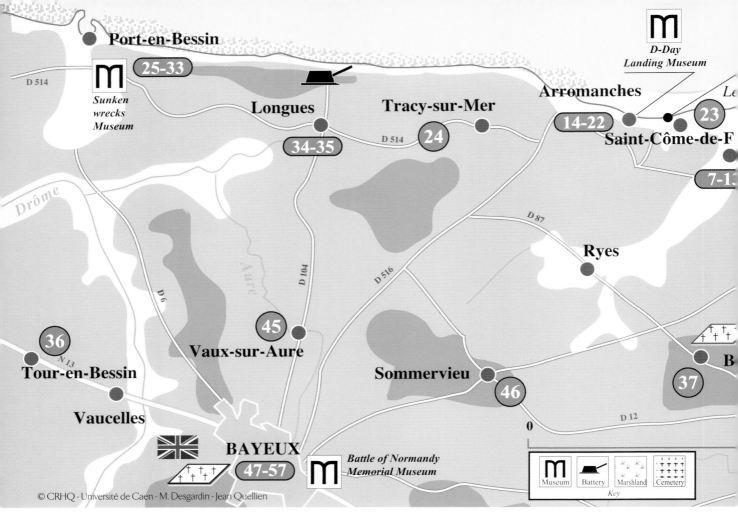

Port-en-Bessin

25-33

M Sunken wrecks Museum

D 514

Longues

34-35

Tracy-sur-Mer

D 514

24

M D-Day Landing Museum

Arromanches

14-22

Saint-Côme-de-F

23

7-13

Drôme

Aure

D 6

D 104

D 516

D 87

Ryes

45

Vaux-sur-Aure

36

N 13

Tour-en-Bessin

Vaucelles

Sommervieu

46

D 12

0

37

B

BAYEUX

47-57

M Battle of Normandy Memorial Museum

| Museum | Battery | Marshland | Cemetery |
Key

© CRHQ · Université de Caen · M. Desgardin · Jean Quellien

■ Post-landing organisation in the Gold Beach sector

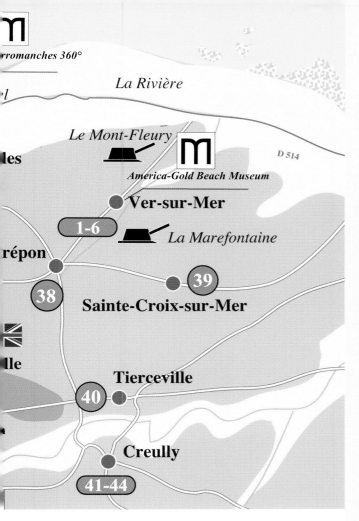

Arromanches 360°

La Rivière

Le Mont-Fleury

M

America-Gold Beach Museum

Ver-sur-Mer

1-6

La Marefontaine

39

38

Sainte-Croix-sur-Mer

Tierceville

40

Creully

41-44

D 514

VER-SUR-MER
1. Monument to the liberators of the village and to the 2nd Hertfordshire Battalion
2. Monument to the 50th Division's Artillery Regiment
3. Plaque on Admiral Ramsey's former HQ
4. Robert Kiln site («Sexton» self-propelled gun).
5. Plaque – Gold Inn (opposite the museum)
6. Plaque – civilian victims (close to the museum)

ASNELLES
7. Plaque – Essex Yeomanry (seaside bunker)
8. Monument to the 231st Brigade
9. 231st Brigade landing observatory (next to the bunker)
10. Artifical harbour anchor (next to the bunker)
11. Monument to the 50th Division's 231st Brigade
12. Monument to the 2nd Battalion South Wales Borderers
13. Monument to the call on the 18th of June 1940 (by General de Gaulle)

ARROMMANCHES
14. Stele – General Stanier (next to the museum)
15. Mulberry "B" monument (idem)
16. Plaque – Royal Logistics Corps (idem)
17. Plaque – Merchant Navy (idem)
18. Plaque – Royal Navy (idem)
19. Stèle- «Lorraine» Group - Free French Air Force
20. Orientation table (plateau)
21. Stele – French Free Air Force (General Fourquet)
22. Monument to the Royal Engineers

SAINT-CÔME-DE-FRESNÉ
23. Plaque – the «Liberation Bells» (church)

TRACY-SUR-MER
24. 6th June stained glass window (church)

PORT-EN-BESSSIN
25. «Essor» Monument
26. Plaque – the cruiser Georges Leygues (town hall)
27. Plaque – the cruiser Montcalm (tourist office)
28. Landings Committee signal monument (pier)
29. Monument to the oil port (pier)
30. Plaque – N°47 Royal Marines Commando (bunker)
31. Stele – N°47 Royal Marines Commando (high school)
32. Monument to N°47 Royal Marines Commando (west cliff)
33. Stele – Captain Cousins (east town entrance)

LONGUES
34. Stele – Aerodrome B-11 (entrance to the battery)
35. 60th Anniversary stele (town hall)

TOUR-EN-BESSIN
36. Stele – Aerodrome A-13

BAZENVILLE
37. Monument to Aerodrome B-2

CRÉPON
38. Green Howards memorial

SAINTE-CROIX-SUR-MER
39. Stele – Aerodrome B-3

TIERCEVILLE
40. «Eros» monument

CREULLY
41. Monument to the 4th/7th Royal Dragoon Guards
42. Plaque – BBC studios (castle)
43. Plaque – Royal Winnipeg Rifles (castle car park)
44. Plaque – de Gaulle's visit to Montgomery (Creullet castle)

VAUX-SUR-AURE
45. Plaque – South Wales Borderers (Aure bridge)

SOMMERVIEU
46. Monument to Aerodrome B-8

BAYEUX
47. General Eisenhower memorial
48. Stele – Sherwood Rangers Yeomanry
49. Stele – Essex Regiment
50. Liberation Monument
51. Column commemorating de Gaulle's speech
52. Plaque – de Gaulle's visit (sous-préfecture)
53. Lorraine Cross (sous-préfecture)
54. Deportation monument
55. Plaque – 50th Division (Rue Le Forestier)
56. Plaque – 56th Brigade (cathedral)
57. British troops stained glass window (cathedral)

■ Canadians enjoying a moment of fraternity at Ver-sur-Mer

Ver-sur-Mer

■ The Mont-Fleury battery bunker

The 69th Brigade landed on the shore at Ver-sur-Mer («King»sector). They made rapid progress across the marshes. The main obstacle to their progress. the fortifications in the coastal hamlet of La Rivière (WN 33). was captured mid-morning. after a tank destroyed the 88mm gun installed in a blockhouse that is still visible on the sea wall. which had been keeping the assailants at bay. The two heavy batteries situated near the village had been reduced to silence by the aerial and naval bombardments. and were quickly captured.

The one at Mont-Fleury. inland from the beach and equipped with four Russian 122mm guns. surrendered without a fight as its garrison was still in shock. The second. at Marefontaine. south of Ver. comprising four 100mm guns in pillboxes. put up little more resistance. A «Sexton» self-propelled gun is on display on the way out of Ver. on the road to Asnelles. at the intersection of the road leading to the beach (avenue Colonel Harper) and the minor road D514. near the monuments to the 2nd Hertfordshire Battalion and the 50th Division's Artillery. Not far from there a house. indicated by a plaque. was used by Admiral Ramsey. commander-in-chief of the Allied navy and the architect of operation Neptune. as his headquarters in Normandy. The America-Gold Museum is located in the centre of the village.

■ Monument in honour of the British liberators

■ «Sexton» self-propelled gun

Asnelles

■ Blockhouse on the sea wall at Asnelles. In the background, vestiges of the artificial harbour

■ Stele - the call of 18th June 1940 .

The 231st Brigade landed without too much difficulty in the «Jig» sector in front of the hamlet of «Les Roquettes». But, in an oblique movement westwards, it ran into strong opposition. The fortifications in the village of Le Hamel (WN 37), which had been spared by the bombardments, inflicted severe losses on the British soldiers. It took them several assaults, support from armoured units and considerable reinforcements to clean out the position, only conquered after a pitched battle in mid-afternoon. A stele, affixed to an imposing seafront blockhouse, recalls that the 88mm gun housed there destroyed six British tanks before being put out of action. On Alexander Stanier square, the monuments to the 2nd South Wales Borderers and to the 231st Brigade are situated

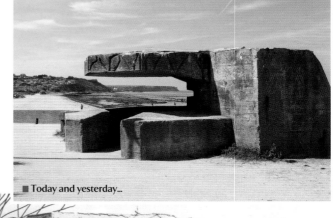

■ Today and yesterday...

beside a memorial surmounted by a Lorraine Cross, evoking the famous speech delivered by General de Gaulle on the 18th of June 1940 calling the French to resist.

It was in Asnelles, where he first reset foot on French soil on the 6th of June 1944, that Maurice Schuman, the former spokesman of the Free French and important post-war political figure, chose to be buried. He died in 1998.

■ 50mm gun on the Asnelles sea wall

■ The artificial harbour in Arromanches

Arromanches

Arromanches was the chosen site for the imposing official ceremony commemorating the 60th
Anniversary of the D-Day Landings. Yet not one
Allied soldier set foot on this beach on the 6th of
June 1944. Indeed, the assault on Arromanches
came overland, not from the sea. Advancing along
the coast from Gold Beach, the 1st Hampshire,
with armoured support, launched their offensive
from Saint-Côme-de-Fresné and took control
of the town on the 6th of June, late afternoon.
A stele, on the town's central square, pays
tribute to General Stanier, commander of the 231st
Brigade, the «liberator of Arromanches».

Arromanches owes its world-wide renown to
its famous artificial harbour, nicknamed «Port
Winston» in honour of Churchill who was behind
the idea. Its story and its operation are fully
described in the D-Day Museum that has been
built on the sea front, on the very spot where a
continuous flow of men, equipment and supplies
surged daily in times past, on their way to reinforce
the armies of liberation.

The remains of this veritable feat of technical
prowess are perfectly visible today, from both the
Tracy-sur-Mer and Saint-Côme-de-Fresné heights.

■ A general view of Arromanches

■ Stele dedicated to the memory of General Stanier

Climbing up from the town of Arromanches following a fairly steep footpath towards Saint-Côme-de-Fresné (to which access is also possible by road) and passing by a Sherman tank, the visitor reaches the top of the cliff to discover the remains of German defensive buildings. The only remaining visible signs of the former Kriegsmarine spotting station, which was destroyed by the aerial bombardments, is a large concrete plinth, the base of a Würzbug FuMO 214 radar installation.

The esplanade on the plateau is dedicated to the memory of General Fourquet, who was commander of the «Lorraine» Group. This unit of the Free French Air Force, flying twin-engined Boston bombers, shared in the bombardment of the German fortifications on the 6th of June. At dawn, one of its planes sank beneath

■ *Würzburg FuMO 214 radar*

■ Orientation table

the waves. The three crew members were the first French airmen killed during the invasion.

An orientation table offers a magnificent viewpoint overlooking the coast and the ocean, and provides substantial information on the artificial harbour. Nearby, visitors can discover the monument erected in tribute to the Royal Engineers and the Arromanches 360° Museum, which houses one of the first circular cinemas to be built in France.

■ Stele dedicated to the memory of General M. Fourquet

■ Radar base

71

■ Jetties on stilts.
The unloading docks were made of large metal platforms linked together by a series of intermediate jetties. Depending on the level of the tide, they slid up and down large 100-foot-high piles, by means of a system of pulleys and winches powered by diesel engines.

A CLOSER LOOK at the ARTIFICIAL HARBOUR IN ARROMANCHES

■ The floating causeways
The floating causeways covered the half mile or more between the docks and dry land, and consisted of metal spans on top of hollow concrete floats, referred to as «Beetles», which endowed the jetties with the capacity to adapt to tidal variations in sea level.

■ Phoenix caissons.
These enormous hollow concrete caissons, weighing between 1,600 and 6,000 tonnes when empty, were destined to form the skeleton of the artificial breakwater providing shelter for the bay. They could measure as much as 200 feet in length, 55 feet in width and be as high as a 5-storey building. Once they arrived on site, they were filled with water by means of a system of sluices and sunk onto the sea bed. Some Phoenix caissons were mounted with turrets armed with anti-aircraft guns.

The costly experience of the raid on Dieppe in 1942 convinced the Allies that any attempt to capture a large port by frontal assault would be in vain. Nevertheless, a large port was absolutely essential for Anglo-American logistics and the success of the invasion.

«As there are no ports available to us, we shall take our own,» declared Winston Churchill defiantly. The idea of the artificial harbours was born. It was then a matter of putting this project, as inspired as it was complex, into practise. The task fell to Lord Mountbatten, chief of combined operations, with the assistance of Admiral Tennant and Commodore Hallet.

The construction of all of the different elements necessary for the construction of two artificial ports, one destined for the American sector off Omaha Beach and the other destined for the British sector off Arromanches, began in England under the code-name «Mulberry».

The prefabricated elements, towed by tugs, crossed the Channel just behind the invasion fleet and their on-site assembly, just like a gigantic Meccano set, began straight after D-Day.

Moored further out from the coast, semi-submerged cruciform metal buoys, the «Bombardons» constituted the first breakwater. The bay, which had a surface area of around 500 hectares (about 1235 acres) was fashioned both by old ships sunk on site, the «Blockships», and large concrete caissons, the «Phoenix».

Unloading docks on stilts linked to the shore by floating causeways were established in the lee of this artificial breakwater.

Hardly was the construction of these two ports complete, when a violent storm hit the Channel from the 19th to the 22nd of June. Mulberry «A» at Omaha, torn to pieces by the crashing waves, had to be abandoned. The salvageable elements were used to repair Mulberry «B» at Arromanches, which had suffered lesser damaged.

The latter was brought back into service, and by the end of June an average 6,000 tonnes of traffic were using it daily. This volume increased to between 15,000 and 20,000 tonnes per day during July and August.

Even if the role played by the artificial harbour at Arromanches has sometimes been overestimated (the Americans, deprived of similar facilities because of the storm from the 19th to the 22nd of June, obtained better results at Omaha), this prodigious technological feat remains one of the keys to the success of the landing operations.

■ Vestiges of a floating causeway

«Port Winston» continued to be used after the capture and reconstruction of Cherbourg and was only abandoned in November 1944.

A simplified plan of Mulberry «B» at Arromanches

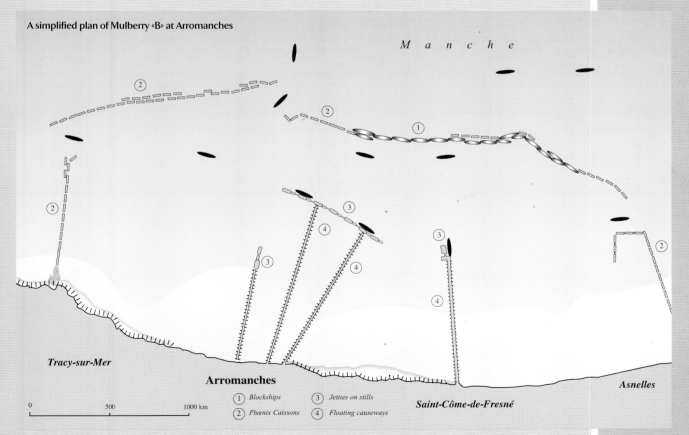

Manche

Tracy-sur-Mer

Arromanches

Saint-Côme-de-Fresné

Asnelles

0   500   1000 km

① Blockships   ③ Jetties on stills
② Phœnix Caissons   ④ Floating causeways

Port-en-Bessin

A plaque affixed to a blockhouse beneath the Tour Vauban, a monument on the cliff top and a stele near the local high school pay tribute to the men from the 47th Royal Marine Commando, the town's liberators. They landed in difficult conditions on the morning of the 6th of June at Asnelles with the mission of advancing parallel to the coast and capturing Port-en-Bessin. They reached the town on the 7th of June, but ran into fierce German resistance, which only weakened in the early hours of the following day.

■ Plaque in tribute to the 47th RMC on the blockhouse at the foot of the Tour Vauban

As did Isigny, Grandcamp and Courseulles, the small port, which was rapidly repaired, played an important role in Allied logistics before the artificial harbours were put into service. Port-en-Bessin was also, along with Sainte-Honorine-des-Pertes (in the American sector), the first fuel terminal on Norman soil, supplied by tankers moored offshore, before the completion of the submarine pipe line linking England to Cherbourg. From there, a system of pipes was used to transport the fuel needed by the Allied armies, whose consumption was considerable. This feat of technological prowess is celebrated by the monument «Essor», situated at the centre of the «Montgomery» roundabout at the entrance to the town, not far from the sunken wrecks museum.

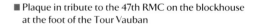
■ Port-en-Bessin in 1944.

Two plaques, one near the town hall and the other near the tourist office, dedicated to the cruisers Montcalm and Georges Leygues, recall the participation of the French navy in the landing operations.

74

Longues-sur-Mer

■ The Longues Battery

The naval battery at Longues, which was built during the first months of 1944, was home to four 155mm guns protected by bunkers. They were situated some 300 yards back from the shore and were connected to the firing command post built on the edge of the cliff. Due to their range of approximately 12 miles, they were a threat for both Omaha and Gold Beaches. Although it had been copiously bombarded before the landings, the Longues battery was still operational and opened fire on the invasion fleet on the morning of the 6th of June. From the moment dawn broke, it engaged in a duel with the American battleship Arkansas, the British cruiser Ajax and the French cruisers Montcalm and Georges Leygues, before being reduced to permanent silence that same evening. The British troops obtained the surrender of the garrison without a fight the following morning.

A visit to the Longues site is exceptionally interesting due to the excellent state of conservation of this heavy battery, the fine restoration performed by volunteers and, above all, as it is the only one in the region still to have its guns.

■ Firing command post

■ Bunker with its 150mm gun.

Crépon

A picturesque bronze statue paying tribute to the Green Howards, representing a «Tommy» taking a moment's respite, has been erected in the town. They landed at Ver at dawn and, before Crépon, had to repel a powerful German counter-offensive led by a dozen anti-tank guns as they advanced in the direction of the RN 13.

A plaque on the plinth pays particular homage to Sergeant E. Hollis for his various acts of bravery on the 6th of June that won him the Victoria Cross, the only one to be awarded on that historic day.

Bazenville

■ Stele marking Aerodrome B-2

In order to be able to give the ground troops sustained support, the construction of aerodromes on Norman soil was a high priority in the Allies' plans. The wide plain south of Caen, a flat and unobstructed area, was ideally suited to this project, but the doughty and lengthy resistance of the Germans outside the Norman capital prevented its realisation. The Allies were constrained to fall back on the Bessin area, a landscape that was less well-suited to the task because of the abundance of trees and hedges that first had to be cut down and flattened to allow the construction of several dozen airfields. The Bazenville aerodrome (named B-2), which was operational as of the 14th of June, was one of the first to be completed in the British sector, along with Sainte-Croix-sur-Mer (B-3). A most original monument, in the shape of a Spitfire wing, has been erected in front of the church in memory of the different squadrons of the 2nd Tactical Air Force based there.

The Commonwealth cemetery at Bazenville was in use only a few days after the invasion. Of the 979 graves there, 630 are British and 326 German.

■ Monument to the «Green Howards».

TO THE MEMORY OF ALL GREEN HOWARDS
WHO FOUGHT AND WHO DIED IN THE SECOND WORLD WAR

REMEMBER
THE 6th JUNE 1944

Creully

■ The castle in Creully

The small town of Creully, situated in the contact zone between the British and Canadian troops, was liberated during the afternoon of the 6th of June.

This mediaeval castle, which had already been occupied by the English during the Hundred Years' War, was home to a BBC studio that broadcast daily radio programmes covering the evolution of the battle in Normandy. As of the 8th of June,

General Montgomery set up his famous tactical command post, a caravan in the grounds of the neighbouring Creullet castle. There, he received visits from various important figures such as Winston Churchill, King George VI and General de Gaulle. On the 23rd, he left and moved to Blay, west of Bayeux, in order to be closer to the Americans.

■ The castle in Creullet

■ 12th June 1944: Montgomery receiving the Prime Minister, Winston Churchill in the grounds of Creullet castle.

Bayeux

■ De Gaulle speaking in front of the sous-préfecture .

■ General de Gaulle in Bayeux on the 14th of June 1944 .

On the morning of the 7th of June. the British entered Bayeux without a fight. It was the first city to be liberated in continental France - the only one until the liberation of Cherbourg - and this peaceful bishopric became a hub of intense activity. The Allies opened a by-pass that went right round the ancient town. the forerunner of the present ring-road. to facilitate the circulation of the heavy traffic that was hindered by the town's narrow streets. Hundreds of refugees from the surrounding countryside flocked to the town. along with the many wounded. a multitude of Allied officers and soldiers taking time off. not forgetting the war correspondents. those dedicated customers of cafés.

The town population suddenly doubled. But. for several months. Bayeux also became the veritable capital of liberated France. It was here. to this little corner of territory freed by the fighting. that General de Gaulle came a few hours after he landed at Courseulles on the 14th of June to affirm the sovereignty of a free France. The enthusiastic welcome given to him by the local population obliged the Allies. like it or not. to recognise his legitimacy and to tolerate the presence of the Prefect. François Coulet. who was charged with the administration of the liberated territories in the name of the provisional government of the French Republic. On the square that bears de Gaulle's name stands a column celebrating the event: other monuments and plaques recall the day. as does the Charles de Gaulle Museum.

Right next to the Battle of Normandy Memorial Museum is the largest British WWII cemetery in France. with 4.648 graves. Opposite the cemetery. on the other side of the boulevard. is a portico-style Memorial on which are engraved the names of 1.808 soldiers whose bodies were never found.

In 1994. for the 50th Anniversary of the landings. the American Battle of Normandy Foundation and the city of Bayeux paid tribute to General Eisenhower. former commander-in-chief of the Allied troops. with the unveiling of a bronze statue. as imposing as it is realistic. in his memory.

Bayeux at a glance

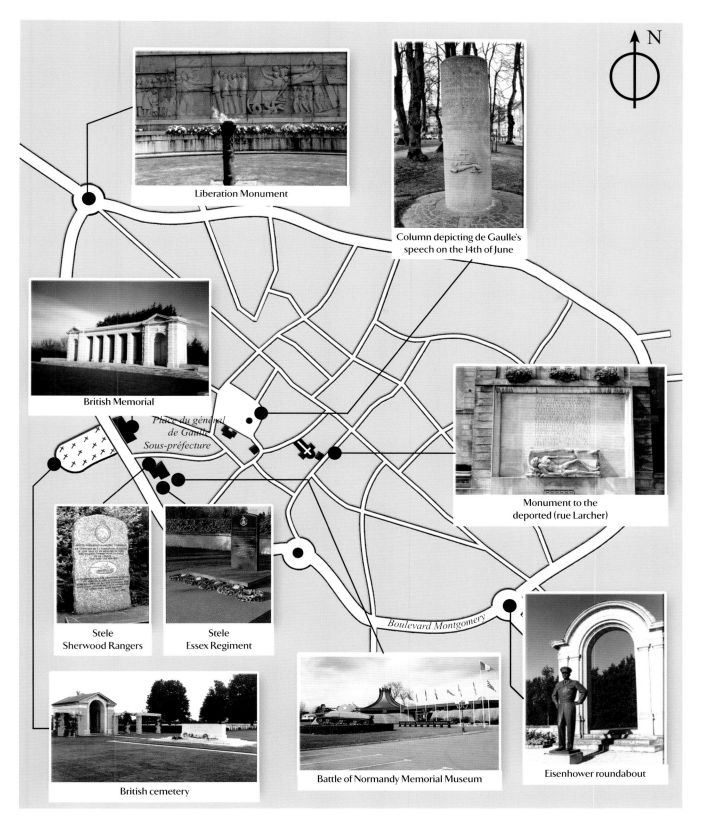

N

Liberation Monument

Column depicting de Gaulle's speech on the 14th of June

British Memorial

Place du général de Gaulle
Sous-préfecture

Monument to the deported (rue Larcher)

Stele Sherwood Rangers

Stele Essex Regiment

Boulevard Montgomery

British cemetery

Battle of Normandy Memorial Museum

Eisenhower roundabout

Canadian troops approaching Juno Beach

Juno Beach

Between the British beaches Gold and Sword, the Juno Beach sector corresponds to the portion of the coast assigned to the Canadians. This sector was occupied by sizeable coastal towns that had become coquettish seaside resorts towards the end of the 19th Century.

There were no heavy-duty batteries here, but a large number of smaller installations lined the shore at regular intervals, housing anti-tank guns and machine guns that were often built onto the sea wall itself, in order to cover the beaches.

The mission to capture Juno Beach fell to General Keller's 3rd Canadian Infantry, with support from the tanks of the 2nd Armoured Brigade and backed up on the left flank by the British 48th Royal Marine Commando.

The sea conditions were to render the Canadians' task extremely difficult. The approach of the barges transporting the first assault wave was hindered both by the heavy swell and the presence of dangerous coastal reefs. When the landings began shortly before 8am, the obstacles on the beach had been largely covered by the rising tide and wreaked havoc among the landing craft. As they shuttled to and fro, many vessels were blown up by the mines set atop stakes driven into the sand.

On the beaches, losses were heavy as the infantry was often left to face the sustained fire from the German positions alone, the arrival of the tanks having been delayed.

But the Canadians were tough warriors. They were all volunteers, as the government in Ottawa, enlightened by the problems it had faced during the First World War, notably the resolute opposition of the French-speaking population, had renounced sending men to fight overseas against their will.

Through sheer force, the first line of the German defences was eventually rent asunder, but the clearing of the villages was to be a lengthy business. The narrowness of the roads, which were often blocked by obstacles, sniper fire, the persistence of pockets of resistance here and there all slowed their progress and caused worrying congestion on the beaches, which were shrinking as the tide rose and soon became clogged with a profusion of heavy equipment.

The forward units, however, lost no time in advancing inland, capturing Saint-Croix, Reviers, Tailleville, Bény, Basly, Pierrepont, Fontaine-Henry, etc.

■ The 3rd Canadian Infantry Division landing at Bernières

By the end of the day, over 21,000 men had been landed and the Canadians had established a solid bridgehead, around eight miles deep. Although they had not managed to reach the main RN 13 road and the aerodrome at Carpiquet, to the west of Caen, they were at least within sight of them. On their right flank, they had linked up with the British who had landed at Gold. On the other hand, to the east of Langrune, where the fighting was still raging as night fell, a corridor separating them from the troops at Sword was still in German hands.

However, on the 7th of June the arrival of the formidable 12th SS «Hitlerjugend» Armoured Division consisting of fanatical young nazis was to bring General Keller's men to an abrupt halt. For over a month, terrible clashes multiplied between the Canadians and the SS outside Caen, characterised by the summary execution of prisoners (notably within the Ardenne Abbey itself). The Canadian landing area, for a long time devoid of a museum, now fortunately has its own: the Juno Beach Centre in Courseulles, inaugurated on the 6th of June 2003.

.

■ Bernières beach on the 6th of June 1944

■ The Basly monument .

■ Monument in memory of the 20 Canadian soldiers executed by the SS in Ardenne Abbey, near Caen .

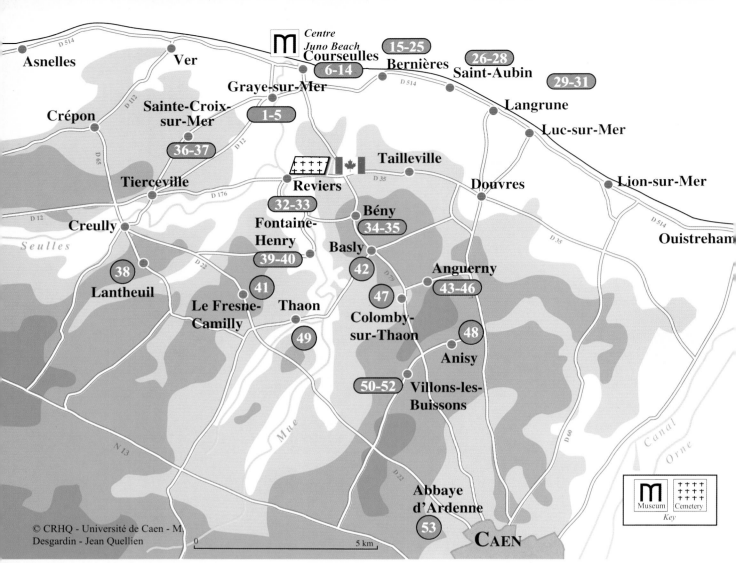

GRAYE-SUR-MER
1. Landing Committee signal monument
2. One Charlie Churchill Tank
3. Plaque – Canadian liberators (church)
4. Inns of Court monument (Brèche de la Vallette)
5. Plaque – Royal Winnipeg Rifles and First Canadian Scottish

COURSEULLES
6. D-Day and return of de Gaulle Memorial
7. Royal Winnipeg Rifles monument
   (Esplanade du Débarquement)
8. Stele - First Canadian Scottish and the Scottish 15th Division
9. Stele - Regina Rifles
10. «La Combattante» memorial
11. Bold amphibious tank
12. Stele - «Nottingham Bridge»
13. Croix de Lorraine
14. Cairn dedicated to Canadian soldiers (Juno Beach Cetnre)

BERNIERES
15. Landing Committee signal monument
16. Memorial to the Queen's Own Rifles
17. Plaque - 5th Hackney Battalion, the Royal Berkshire Regiment and N°8 Beach Group
18. «La Chaudière» Regiment memorial
19. Plaque - Fort Garry Horse
20. Stele of Remembrance 1944 - 1994 (Bernières remembers)
21. Plaque - Journalists' HQ
22. Cairn in memory of Canadian soldiers (tourist office)
23. Plaque – North Nova Scotia (sea rescue station)
24. Stained glass window (church)
25. Monument to the 14th Field Regiment (Route de Bény)

SAINT-AUBIN
26. Monument to the Fort Garry Horse
27. Monument to the «North Shore» and N°48 Royal Marine Commando
28. Monument dedicated to the fallen from various Canadian units, the town's civilian victims and Maurice Duclos' Mission.

LANGRUNE
29. Monument to N°48 Royal Marine Commando
30. «Work of War» monument
31. Plaque - N°48 Royal Marine Commando (town hall lobby)

REVIERS
32. Plaque - Cameron Highlanders of Ottawa (cemetery)
33. Stele - Regina Rifles

BÉNY
34. Stele - Aerodrome B-4
35. Stele - «La Chaudière» Regiment

SAINTE-CROIX-SUR-MER
36. Stele - Aerodrome B-3
37. Plaque in memory of the Canadian soldiers killed on the 6th of June 1944 (cemetery)

LANTHEUIL
38. Stele - Aerodrome B-9

FONTAINE-HENRY
39. Plaque to the memory of the Canadians who died liberating the village (church)
40. Monument to the Canadian liberators

LE FRESNE-CAMILLY
41. Monument with plaques commemorating Aerodrome B-5, the Royal Winnipeg Rifles and the Canadian Scottish

BASLY
42. Monument to the Canadian liberators

ANGUERNY
43. Stele - «La Chaudière» Regiment
44. Plaque - Queen's Own Rifles
45. Monument to the Fort Garry Horse
46. Stele – Captain Gauvin from the "La Chaudière" Regiment

COLOMBY-SUR-THAON
47. Stele to the «La Chaudière» Regiment

ANISY
48. Monument du Queen's Own Rifles

THAON
49. Stele to the Fort Garry Horse

VILLONS-LES-BUISSONS
50. Monument - «Coin de l'Enfer»
51. Monument to the Norwegian troops
52. Stele - Aerodrome B-16

ARDENNE ABBEY
53. Monument in memory of the Canadian soldiers executed by the SS

Graye-sur-Mer

■ D-Day Committee signal monument

■ Remains of a Bunker that once housed a 75mm gun

On the left, the Winnipeg Rifles and the 1st Canadian Scottish landed at the dunes down from Graye without sustaining too much damage and rapidly secured the village, situated a short way inland. The only resistance they met with was from a detachment of Russian gunners dug into the Vaux castle sanatorium. Without wasting a second, the Canadians drove onward in the direction of Sainte-Croix. Over the days following D-Day, several important figures crossed the sand on the beach at Graye, including the British Prime Minister, Winston Churchill, who Montgomery received on the 12th of June, and King George VI, four days later.

The Churchill tank that can be seen in the dunes, not far from the Landing Committee monument and the Lorraine Cross in Courseulles, has a singular history.

■ The Churchill A.V.R.E. tank
This «Fascine» tank belonging to the 79th Armoured Division, which landed with the assault troops, sank into a marsh behind the dunes at Graye. The engineers immediately built a metal bridge over it to enable vehicles to pass. It was later buried under rubble and disappeared for many years under a metalled road. In 1976, the village mayor decided to disinter the tank, in the presence of the two surviving members of its crew, and to have it restored

Courseulles-sur-Mer

■ Monument to the Royal Winnipeg Rifles.

■ Amphibious «DD» tanks were equipped with a dual pro-pulsion system (Duplex Drive), enabling them to move both in the sea (using propellers) and on land. The chassis, which was made watertight, was surrounded by a hull around which was attached a high skirt of pliable material that enabled it - theoretically - to float. But on the 6th of June, because of the heavy weather, many of them sank before reaching the shore. This was the case of the «Bold» tank, fished from the bottom 27 years later, restored to its original condition and dedicated to Sergeant Léo Gariépy who led the assault on the beach at Courseulles at the head of the «B» squadron of the Ist Hussars.

Courseulles, a small port renowned for its oyster production, was without doubt the most solidly fortified section of the Juno Beach sector. There were at least a dozen anti-tank guns on either side of the Seulles estuary, not counting the numerous machine gun nests and mortar emplacements, so the task facing the men of the Winnipeg Rifles and the Regina Rifles was a tough one. They acquitted themselves of their task, albeit with heavy losses, and were in control of the area by the middle of the morning.

Apart from the various monuments erected in tribute to Courseulles' liberators, most of which are located on Charles de Gaulle square or near it, several relics, including a Bold amphibious tank and a German 50mm anti-tank gun, recall the fighting in 1944.

■ Croix de Lorraine symbolising De Gaulle's return to France on the 14th of June 1944.

■ Monument to the "La Combattante" torpedo boat .

From the 8th of June onwards. the port. reconstructed and protected offshore by a Gooseberry (a screen of old ships scuttled on site) was used to land men and equipment. sometimes as much as 2.000 tonnes per day.

It was on the beach at Courseulles that General de Gaulle set foot in the early afternoon on the 14th of June. having been brought from England by «La Combattante». a Free French navy torpedo boat that had been on the same spot eight days previously as supporting fire-power for the invading Canadian troops. From there. in the company of his closest colleagues. the General went about criss-crossing the whole bridgehead area with the intention of affirming the authority of the provisional government of the French Republic. The memory of this event is recalled by several monuments. of which the most spectacular and most recent is the immense Lorraine Cross erected in 1990 on the dune at the territorial limit of Graye beach.

■ Courseulles beach in June 1944 .

Bernières-sur-Mer

■ The large villa visible in the background of the 1944 photograph, near the signal monument .

Bernières found itself in the centre of the 8th Brigade's assault sector («Nan White»). The Queen's Own Rifles of Canada Regiment suffered heavy losses before smashing through the German defences. One of the companies lost half of its men in the hundred yards of beach separating them from the sea wall. The famous «La Chaudière» Regiment that was composed mostly of French-speaking Canadians landed here, too, in the second wave. Their mission was to rid the village of the snipers lurking there. The locals discovered to their astonishment that these «Tommies» spoke French.

Because of the delays in getting the troops moving inland, the beach was soon blocked with men and equipment, above all after the arrival of a brigade of reinforcements. General Keller, commander of the 3rd Division, set up his HQ in Bernières around midday. The British and Canadian war correspondents chose themselves a hotel from which to send their first reports. Nowadays, the hotel has become a private house (N°228, Rue du Régiment de la Chaudière) and there is a memorial plaque on its façade. Most of the commemorative memorials have been erected on the sea front on the Place du Canada, where the WN 28 previously stood. This system of defences, nicknamed «La Cassine» by the Canadians, was the focal point of the fighting in 1944.

■ Bernières locals meet with their French-speaking Canadian "cousins" from the "La Chaudère" Regiment

■ Commemorative monuments, Place du Canada; in the insert, the « La Chaudière » Regiment monument .

Saint-Aubin-sur-Mer

■ 50mm anti-tank gun on the sea wall at Saint-Aubin

Well before the landings. Saint-Aubin had been the scene of an important event. During the night of the 3rd to the 4th of August 1940. two Free France agents. Maurice Duclos («Saint-Jacques») and Alexandre Beresnikoff («Corvisart») began one of the very first reconnaissance missions undertaken in occupied France here.

Four years later. the men of the North Shore landed here. with support from the Fort Garry Horse and flanked on their left by the British Royal Marines of N°48 Commando. The assailants on this section of «Nan Red» were given a particularly rough reception by the German defences. notably by a 50mm gun housed in a bunker that is still in place on the sea wall. Several monuments have been erected near the bunker on the Square des Canadiens. On either side of the memorial to the memory of the North Shore. and N°48 Royal Marine Commando. two stelae resembling open books bear the names of the soldiers of various units who fell at Saint-Aubin. and those of the local civilian victims. They also evoke the «Saint-Jacques» mission.

■ Commemorative monuments, Square des Canadiens

Langrune-sur-Mer

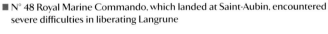
N° 48 Royal Marine Commando, which landed at Saint-Aubin, encountered severe difficulties in liberating Langrune

The monument paying tribute to N°48 Royal Marine Commando was erected on the Place du 6 Juin at the very place where a group of houses the Germans had transformed into a formidable fortification formerly stood. Having landed in particularly adverse conditions to the east of Saint-Aubin, the British commandos' mission consisted in moving along the coast in order to make contact with Sword Beach. They were held up for a long time at Langrune, where they were obliged to fight road by road, house by house, before wresting definitive mastery of the village from the Germans on the 7th of June at the beginning of the afternoon. By then, only 340 men of the 630 engaged in the battle on the morning of the 6th of June were still fit to fight. Near the N°48 Commando monument, there is an original piece of sculpture by Dominique Colas, «Work of War», made using compressed weapons and military equipment.

■ *«Work of War», by the sculptor Dominique Colas.*
The monument to N°48 Commando is in the background

CLOSE UP LOOK at the COMMONWEALTH CEMETERIES

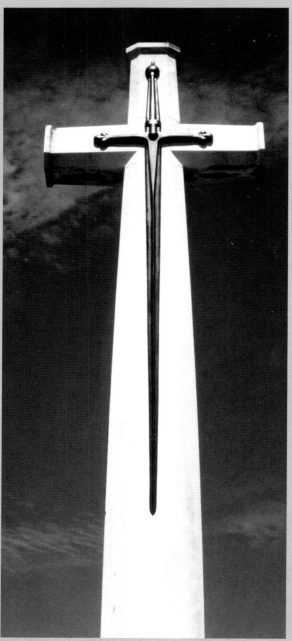

■ The Cross of Sacrifice

By virtue of a very ancient custom in the British Army, the bodies of soldiers killed in wartime are not repatriated but are buried where they fell. Consequently, cemeteries are sometimes very small (47 graves in Chouains), and the number of Commonwealth cemeteries in Normandy is high (16 British, 2 Canadian), not counting a few hundred graves in local village graveyards throughout the region. Another original aspect is the frequent presence of graves of soldiers of other nationalities, including Germans (a third of the graves at Bazenville).

■ The Stone of Remembrance
Each of these monuments, only present in the largest Cemeteries, bears the inscription, «Their name liveth for evermore».

The Commonwealth cemeteries all share the same general architectural design, established during WWI. The presence of trees, flower beds, pergolas and a border with flowers running along the foot of the graves give the impression of being in a garden as much as being in a cemetery.

The composition is simple and is organised around a wide central alley. A Cross of Sacrifice set with a bronze sword stands in all the cemeteries. Commemorative ceremonies take place at the foot of these crosses. Open-air altar-shaped monuments, the Stones of Remembrance, have been set in the largest cemeteries. Depending on their size, the Commonwealth cemeteries include one or two reception buildings in which are kept the register and the visitors' book, a map and a text describing operations during the Battle of Normandy. Each grave is marked by a rectangular white Italian limestone stele, with a slightly rounded top.

■ **Canadian cemetery in Reviers**
The Canadian soldiers killed during the Battle of Normandy were for the most part buried in two cemeteries, one in Reviers (2,049 graves) and the other in Cintheaux (2,958 graves) situated between Caen and Falaise.

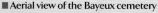

■ **Aerial view of the Bayeux cemetery**

■ **Douvres cemetery**

■ The grave of soldier Ouellet (Reviers)
Each stele is engraved with the emblem of the weapon or the regiment to which the deceased belonged. In the case of Canadians, this is replaced by a maple leaf, and a fern for New Zealanders. A personalised inscription chosen by the bereaved family figures beneath the deceased's name.

■ The artillery battery on Riva-Bella beach

Sword Beach

Initially, the landing sector defined by the Allies reached no further east than Courseulles. Eisenhower and Montgomery convinced in extending it as far as the river Orne. Thus it was that Sword Beach appeared to the east of Juno Beach; it theoretically stretched from Langrune to Ouistreham. Considering the risks weighing on a direct assault against the powerful coastal defences at Ouistreham, and the impossibility of landing opposite Lion and Luc-sur-Mer because of the coastal reefs, the site chosen for the offensive was a relatively narrow strip between Hermanville and Colleville.

■ Insignia of the British 3rd Division

It was here that General Rennie's British 3rd Division landed with support from amphibious and special tanks. On the flanks, it had support in the person of the «Green Berets», two special commando brigades. To the east, the 1st Brigade, commanded by Lord Lovat, a Scottish nobleman never without his loyal piper, the famous Bill Millin, had been entrusted with the mission of heading left and capturing Ouistreham side-on. At the other extremity, the 4th Brigade (N°s 41 and 46 Commando) were to take Lion-sur-Mer and Luc-sur-Mer.

The 8th Brigade of the 3rd Division, which landed at a spot aptly named «La Brèche» (The Breach), succeeded in breaking through the Atlantic Wall, in spite of doughty opposition. It now fell to the 185th Brigade to make the most of the situation in carrying out a mission of capital importance: seizing Caen before nightfall. However, the overcrowding of the beach, resulting both from the disorder caused by the German

■ N°45 Royal Marine Commando. Insert: Insignia of the British Commandos

■ The 21st Panzer counter-attacking

■ The British troops assemble before the assuault inland

artillery fire and the narrowness of the roads that held up the flow of troops inland, were already jeopardising the accomplishment of their objective. The resistance put up by the fortified positions around the village of Colleville, and the counter-attack launched by the 21st Panzer in mid-afternoon on the Périers-sur-le-Dan ridge, made the problem ever more complicated. The lack of decisiveness of certain high-ranking British officers, who were more concerned with consolidating their hold on the ground than forging ahead, did the rest.

When the leading elements of the 3rd Division finally drew near to Caen, in the early evening, it was already too late. They were pinned down by the defensive barrier established by the Germans. It was to take a month of unstinting and violent fighting before they could enter the city, which had been devastated by the battle.

Meanwhile, Lord Lovat's 1st Special Brigade had reached the Bénouville and Ranville bridges and joined up with the paratroopers.

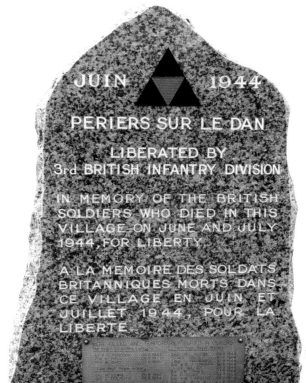

■ Stele - British 3rd Division
in Périers-sur-le-Dan .

Hermanville-sur-Mer

■ The Place du Cuirassé Courbet

The British 3rd Infantry Division landed on Queen Beach, a sector principally situated in front of Hermanville. Whereas the South Lancashire did not meet with particular difficulties on Queen White, the same could not be said of the East Yorkshire which landed on Queen Red. Nevertheless, Hermanville was cleared around 10am and reinforcements could start landing in their turn.

Offshore from Hermanville, and in order to facilitate operations on the beach, the Allies quickly established a Gooseberry, a breakwater constituted of old ships scuppered on site. Among them was the venerable French battleship Courbet (launched in 1911), which had fled to England in 1940, and whose carcass is still at the bottom of the sea. The French tricolour flag that was flying from its masthead today embellishes one of the town hall's walls. A stele reminds us that when the commander of the Courbet, Captain Wietzel, reached land, he picked up a handful of French earth to take back to General de Gaulle. The precious packet is now kept in Colombey-les-Deux-Églises. Various commemorative monuments have been erected in front of the tourist office on the Place du Cuirassé Courbet. One of them pays tribute to the Allied pioneers who are said to have landed on the beach ... on the 5th of June at 2300 hours: an affirmation that causes a few historians' eyebrows to be raised. Near a horizontal slab bearing the insignia of the 3rd Division, two other monuments salute the unit's artillery and one of its regiments, the South Lancashire, which liberated the village. The "Le Matelot" monument was inaugurated in June 2004 by King Harald V of Norway in homage to the Norwegian seamen. During the summer months, the tourist office displays an exhibition of photographs and various objects including a scale model of the Sword Beach Gooseberry.

■ The Hermanville Gooseberry; in the centre, the Courbet

■ A Bren carrier in front of the Hotel de la Brèche

A Cromwell tank is on display not far from there, towards Colleville. Right next to it, facing the sea, a monument salutes the decisive role played by the seamen in the success of the invasion. The division's HQ and a field hospital were set up in the castle grounds (now the town hall), in the centre of the village, some small way inland. Two plaques, one on either side of the entrance gate, remind us of this. Across the road, a small stele pays tribute to Harold Pickersgill, «Honorary citizen of the village». Pickersgill was one of those who secretly worked in Britain on the drawing of maps, based on information gleaned from aerial photographs and the Resistance, for the purposes of the invasion. In 1944, he obtained permission to land at Hermanville, a sector he knew well, as he had mapped it. He married a French woman after the war and settled in Normandy, where he died in 1998. On the little square near the church, the visitor will find a strange object. For having supplied the troops with the water they needed, a plaque informs us that the Mare Saint-Pierre well has the honour of having been included on the roll of the British army. From this square, a small path leads to the military cemetery and its 1,005 graves, for the most part those of British soldiers killed during the landing at Sword Beach or during the 3rd Division's advance towards Caen.

■ The Mare Saint-Pierre well

■ Monument paying tribute to the 150,000 seamen who took part in the landings.

99

Colleville-Montgomery

Lieutenant Commander Kieffer's French marine fuseliers and their British comrades of N°4 Commando landed on Colleville Beach, at the western extremity of Queen Red. At the edge of the beach, a bas-relief sculpture symbolically facing an impressive blockhouse is dedicated to their memory.

A granite stele, also dedicated to their memory, indicates the beginning of the Avenue du N°4 Commando, situated at the meeting point of Colleville and Ouistreham beaches. Opposite it stands one of the oldest monuments commemorating the landings. It was erected on the 6th of June 1945 on the spot where the first Allied soldiers to die during the assault were provisionally buried and pays homage to the men of Kieffer's commando unit and to the British troops. A special mention is dedicated to their commander, General Montgomery, whose name has been joined to that of the village, as requested by the town council as a pledge of gratitude. Crossing the coast road,

the visitor will discover a very lifelike statue of the famous «Monty», unveiled by Prince Edward, Duke of Kent in 1996 in the middle of a square.

The village of Colleville, situated a little over a mile inland, was flanked by several fortified positions. Just west of the village, the WN 16 (code-named Morris by the British) housed a battery of four 100mm guns. The battery had a Polish gun crew who put up little resistance, and it fell around 1300 hours. The same could not be said of the subsequent WN 17, code-named "Hillman" by the Allies. Situated on a mound overhanging the coast, it was used as the HQ of the 736th Regiment of the 716th German Infantry Division, in charge of defending the sector. Established as of 1942, it was equipped with a dozen concrete structures, buried at a depth four metres underground. These blockhouses, one

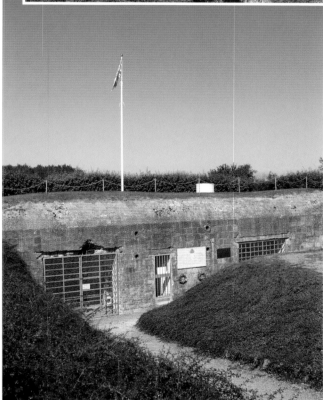

■ Commandos from the 1st Special Brigade landing

■ Bunkers on the Hillman site

of which was surmounted by an armoured turret, comprised a control room, a transmission room, kitchens and quarters for the garrison to rest... linked together by a network of trenches. The entire perimeter was surrounded with barbed-wire, minefields and was solidly defended by machine gun posts and anti-tank guns. It stubbornly resisted the men from the 1st Suffolk Battalion, who were charged with capturing it. The initial assault was postponed to the afternoon of the 6th of June and Hillman only fell the following morning. Its late capture considerably delayed the capture of Caen. After the

■ Bas-relief paying tribute to the Commandos

war, the site was abandoned and the structures became dumping grounds. Since the early 1990's, an association, "Les amis du Suffolk Regiment", helped by the town of Colleville, has undertaken to clear the shelters in order to restore the Hillman site and to open it to visitors. One of the blockhouses has been converted into a visitor centre.

■ Stele in memory of the first Allied soldiers to fall on the 6th of June 1944

A LA GLOIRE
DES TROUPES DE LEURS MAJESTES BRITANNIQUES
LE ROI ET LA REINE
ET EN MÉMOIRE DES PREMIERS ALLIÉS TOMBES LE 6 JUIN 1944
DONT LA DÉPOUILLE SACRÉE A REPOSÉ A CET ENDROIT
FIRST BRITISH GRAVES
SUR CETTE PLACE A L'AUBE DU 6 JUIN 1944 LES TROUPES DU
MARÉCHAL MONTGOMERY ET LE COMMANDO FRANÇAIS DU
CAPITAINE KIEFFER MIRENT LES PREMIERS LE PIED SUR LA TERRE
DE FRANCE
AVEC UN COURAGE ET UNE TENACITÉ ADMIRABLES, AU PRIX DE LOURDS ET
SANGLANTS SACRIFICES ILS S'ACCROCHÈRENT AU SOL ET PERMIRENT AINSI
LA LIBERATION DE TOUT LE CONTINENT
CE MARBRE A ÉTÉ APPOSÉ EN HOMMAGE DE GRATITUDE ET DE PIEUSE
RECONNAISSANCE PAR LA POPULATION DE COLLEVILLE POUR GLORIFIER ET
IMMORTALISER TOUS CEUX QUI RÉPONDANT A L'ESPOIR SACRÉ DE TOUT
UN PEUPLE ONT QUITTÉ FAMILLE ET PATRIE POUR CHASSER
L'OPPRESSEUR ALLEMAND
C'EST POUR RAPPELER AUX GÉNÉRATIONS FUTURES LES EXPLOITS DE
CES HEROS SUBLIMES PERSONNIFIÉS PAR UN CHEF VALEUREUX
QUE COLLEVILLE A VOULU UNIR A SON NOM
CELUI DU MARÉCHAL MONTGOMERY

COLLEVILLE-MONTGOMERY 6 JUIN 1945

■ General Bernard L. Montgomery

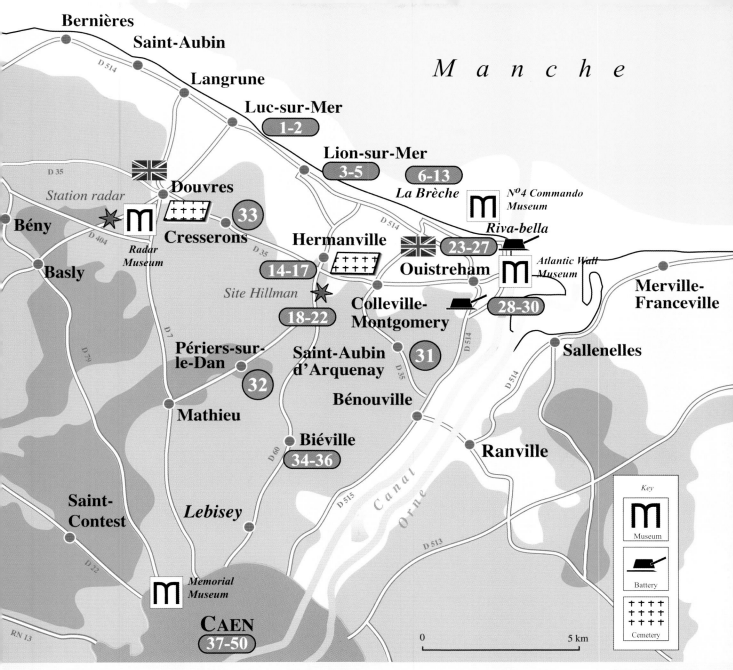

LUC-SUR-MER
1. Monument to the Allied raid in September 1941 and the liberation of the town
2. Monument to General Leclerc and the 2nd Armoured Division (Place Leclerc)

LION-SUR-MER
3. Monument to N°41 Commando (sundial)
4. Monument to the 77th Royal Engineers Squadron
5. Monument - 40th Anniversary of the liberation of Lion

HERMANVILLE "LA BRÈCHE"
6. Stele - South Lancashire
7. Monument to the 3rd Division Royal Artillery
8. Liberation monument
9. "Le Matelot" monument, dedicated to the Danish seamen
10. D-Day stained glass window (La Brèche chapel)
11. Admiral Wietzel memorial (Boulevard de la 3ème Division)
12. Monument to Allied seamen
13. Plaque in memory of the staff officers of the 9th Brigade (Rue du Clos Moulin)

HERMANVILLE BOURG
14. Plaque - Mare Saint-Pierre well
15. Plaque - 3rd Division HQ (town hall)
16. Plaque - Field hospital (town hall)
17. Stele in memory of Harold Pickersgill (village hall)

COLLEVILLE-MONTGOMERY
18. Statue of General Montgomery
19. N°4 Commando monument
20. Provisional cemetery monument
21. Plaque – 1st Battalion of the Suffolk Regiment (Hillman site)
22. Plaque – Private J.R. Hunter (Hillman site)

OUISTREHAM RIVA-BELLA
23. «La Flamme» monument
24. Stele - Lieutenant Commander Kieffer
25. Monument to the Royal Navy seamen and the Royal Marines (port)
26. Plaques - N°4 Commando and tribute to Captain Lion (Rue Pasteur)
27. Stele in memory of Commandos Hubert. Labas, Lemoigne & Letang (Boulevard Churchill)

OUISTREHAM BOURG
28. Commandos and Scottish 51st Division stained glass window (church)
29. Landing Committee signal Monument and N°4 Commando plaque
30. Royal Hussars monument

SAINT-AUBIN-D'ARQUENAY
31. Monument to the commandos of the 1st Special Service Brigade

PÉRIERS-SUR-LE-DAN
32. Stele - 3rd Infantry Division

CRESSERONS
33. Stele - 22nd Dragoons

BIEVILLE
34. Monument to the Allied combatants
35. Stele – Royal Norfolk
36. Stele – 18th June 1940

CAEN
37. Stele - 50th anniversary of the liberation by the Canadians
38. Stele - Canadian soldiers who fell for the liberation of Caen
39. Monument to the Stormont. Dundas and Glengarry Highlanders
40. Monument to the British 3rd Division
41. Plaque - memorial to those shot on the 6th of June
42. Monument to those shot on the 6th of June
43. Monument to the people of Caen who were deported or shot
44. Stele - Patriotic ceremony on the 9th of July 1944
45. Civilian victims' square and monument
46. Monument to Caen's ordeal
47. Plaque - Refugees in Saint-Étienne church
48. Plaque - Emergency teams
49. Stele - General de Gaulle
50. Wall of remembrance – American garden - Caen Memorial for Peace

Ouistreham

■ «The Flame» monument. On the left is Lieutenant Commander Kieffer's stele.
The stones in the foreground bear the names of the French commandos killed on the beach

The peaceful seaside resort of Ouistreham-Riva-Bella, controlling the Orne estuary and the entrance to the canal, had been turned into a *Stützpunkt* (fortified position) by the Germans. The majority of the seafront villas had been knocked down to make way for a veritable entrenched camp, bristling with bunkers, armoured shelters, guns, machine gun nests and mortars.

■ One of the 155mm guns in place on Riva Bella beach

■ Remains of «dragon's teeth» anti-tank defences

One of the most powerful batteries on the Lower Normandy coast was established here on the beach itself. It was equipped with six 155mm guns set in concrete vats. Nevertheless, lacking pillboxes to protect them from airborne attacks, the guns had been transferred inland shortly before the landings. Whereas not a trace of the battery remains, nor of the many anti-tank positions that covered the site, there are several remains of smaller defensive constructions behind the cabins lining the beach.

Finally, the imposing firing command post, nearly 60 feet high, has escaped demolition. It now houses the Atlantic Wall Museum.

■ A «Tobruk» shelter

To complete the system, another battery had been established south of the village, near the water tower. Two bunkers are still in existence, but access to them is not easy.

The men from N°4 Commando, who landed at Colleville just after 0730, had the difficult task of capturing Ouistreham. Lieutenant commander Philippe Kieffer's 177 marines, the only Frenchmen active on the ground on D-Day, spear-headed this deployment. When they regrouped in the ruins of a holiday camp, they had already lost 40 of their comrades, dead or wounded, on the beach.

Their losses were no less severe as they advanced through Ouistreham, capturing fortified positions one by one, under sniper fire. While the British were vigorously battling their way to conquering the battery on the beach, the Frenchmen reached the area round the Casino. Although no offence is intended to Daryl Zanuck, the building looked nothing like its depiction in the film «The Longest Day» in 1944... because it had been demolished in 1943 to clear the firing area. Only the foundations had been conserved, and the building transformed into a fortification. Tank support was needed before the position fell around 0930 hours.

The firing command post remained for a while in German hands in rather unusual conditions. Having repelled a first assault, which had not been followed up, its occupants were careful not to show themselves, in the hope of being forgotten. It was not until the 10th of June that, by chance, a British patrol tumbled to their ploy on attempting to enter the bunker and obtained the surrender of the 53-man garrison without difficulty.

Obviously, Kieffer's commandos are highly honoured in Ouistreham today. The stele dedicated to their leader, near «The Flame» monument (symbol of the French Resistance), symbolically erected on a former armoured machine gun shelter, is complemented by a plaque affixed to the Landing Committee signal monument, situated on the roundabout at the entrance to the town, not forgetting the N°4 Commando museum.

■ Monument paying tribute to the Royal Navy crews and Commandos

■ 50mm anti-tank gun defending the Douvres radar station.

CLOSE UP LOOK at the DOUVRES RADAR STATION

■ The «Würzburg» radar reinstalled on the site at Douvres in 1994.

In 1942, the Germans built a large Lüftwaffe radar detection station west of the town of Douvres on a plateau about 3 miles from the shore, which was code-named «Distelfink» (Goldfinch). It covered nearly 10 hectares and was composed of two installations, one on each side of the road to Bény. The northern part was equipped with a «Wasserman» radar, used for long-range spotting of the surrounding airspace.

The southern part, which was larger, included two medium-range Freya radar and two parabolic Würzburg-Riese dishes; the whole station was completed by many partially buried concrete buildings, for use by the garrison or as munitions stores and a large bunker with twenty-odd rooms housing the operations room and command post. It was solidly fortified, and constituted a veritable entrenched camp, surrounded by minefields, barbed wire and trenches, defended by anti-tank guns and machine gun nests.

■ The "Wasserman" radar antenna (destroyed by aerial bombardment before the landings) measured over 130 feet in height.

During the decisive hours, the Douvres radar station was to prove incapable of fulfilling the surveillance task for which it had been built, as it had been copiously bombarded before the invasion, as had all the stations in the Seine Bay and on the North Sea coast and, like them, was moreover subjected to intense jamming during the night of the 5th to the 6th of June. Its defensive system remained, nevertheless, virtually intact.

So the Canadian and British troops decided to skirt the obstacle and move on towards Caen without wasting any time. The «Distelfink» position, defended by 230 men, was thus to remain isolated behind the Allied

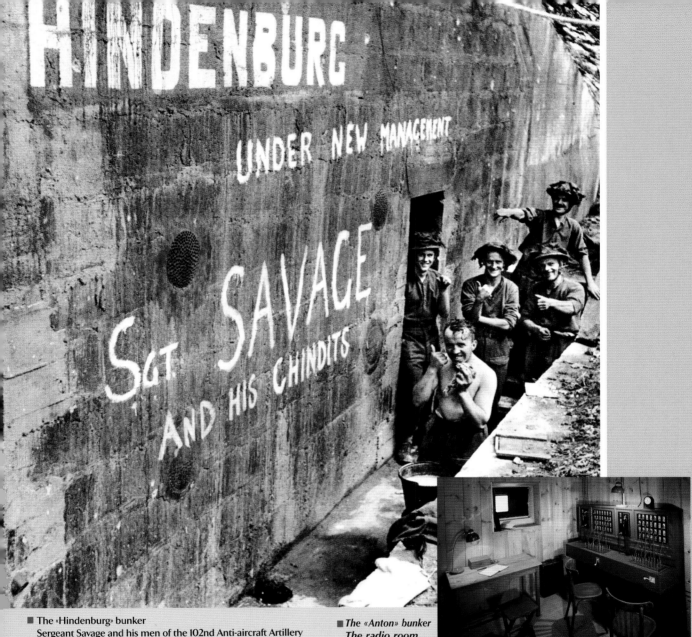

The «Hindenburg» bunker
Sergeant Savage and his men of the 102nd Anti-aircraft Artillery Regiment captured the «Hindenburg» bunker.

The «Anton» bunker
The radio room

lines and held out for twelve days against the commandos who were trying to overrun it. It finally surrendered on the 17th of June, following a by-the-book offensive led by the special tanks of the 79th Armoured Division.

As part of the D-Day 50th Anniversary celebrations, part of the Douvres radar station site was renovated, including the opening of a museum in the main bunker («Anton»). A Würzburg-Riese telescope, identical to the ones with which «Distelfink» was equipped in 1944 and retrieved from the observatory in Paris, has been installed on site.

The «Anton» bunker
Reconstitution of a room reserved for the garrison's barracks.

Lion-sur-Mer

The shore at Lion-sur-Mer and Luc-sur-Mer being maladapted to landing operations, both these seaside resorts had to be captured by means of assaults launched from Hermanville to the east and Langrune to the west. Arriving from Hermanville, the N°41 Royal Marines Commando experienced the greatest of difficulties in dislodging the Germans from Lion, in spite of support from tanks and supporting fire from the navy. During the evening of the 7th, however, following the capture of the last enemy positions, the Royal Marines linked up with N°48 Commando in Luc-sur-Mer, thus giving the British control of the whole coastal sector from Port-en-Bessin to Ouistreham. The previous day, taking advantage of the delayed linking up with the Canadians, a detachment of tanks from the 21st Panzer had succeeded in infiltrating the lines and reaching the beach between Lion and Luc around 8pm. Finding themselves isolated, this unit decided to retreat without having turned the situation to their advantage. The spectacular monument to N°41 Commando erected on the Route de Luc takes the unusual form of a large sundial. At the foot of the edifice, a plaque recalls the sequence of events on the 6th of June including an extract from a speech by President

■ N°41 Royal Marine Commando Monument

Roosevelt evoking the fundamental liberties that had to be protected from dictatorships.

Luc-sur-Mer

«Passer-by, stand and reflect» can be read on the stele standing on the seafront promenade. Two events are evoked there. First of all, the raid during the night of the 28th of September 1941 by a small Allied commando unit on reconnaissance. The second recalls the liberation of the village on the 7th of June by the N°46 Royal Marines Commando, who had landed that same morning at Saint-Aubin, after fierce fighting to capture a small group of houses the Germans had fortified at the hamlet called «Le Petit Enfer» («Little Hell»). After the liberation of Luc, the Hotel Belle Plage (since transformed into seafront housing), requisitioned by the British Army, became a place of rest and relaxation for the men of the 3rd Infantry Division during the Battle of Normandy.

■ The monument at Luc-sur-Mer

■ The devastated city of Caen a few months after its liberation

Caen

Caen, the main town in the Calvados department, and the largest town in Lower Normandy, had a population of 60,000 in 1944, and was to suffer particularly brutally from the conflict that summer. When the fighting was done, three quarters of the «anvil of victory», in the words of the British historian Alexander McKee, had been destroyed and the city was mourning 2,000 civilian dead.

In the Allies' plans, Caen should have been captured on the evening of the 6th of June but, because they had been held up as they moved south from the coast, neither the Canadians nor the British managed to achieve their objective. Over the following days, the Germans established a solid defensive barrier in front of the town, with support from several armoured divisions, including the formidable 12th Panzer SS «Hitlerjugend».

After a terrible siege, the town was to wait until the 9th of July for its left bank to be liberated, and ten days longer for the right bank to follow suite.

Meanwhile, Caen had suffered incessant artillery fire and a series of lethal aerial bombardments. The first of these, on the 6th of June at around 1330 hours, was aimed at the bridges over the Orne. It was badly targeted and destroyed the town centre between the castle and the river, costing the lives of 600 people. On the night of the 6th to the 7th of June, it had become a question of deliberately destroying the town to prevent German armoured reinforcements from driving through it. The last major bombardment, on the 7th of July, north of the town, heralded the final Anglo-Canadian assault. From the 6th of June onwards, a large part of the population

■ A Canadian patrol in Rue Saint-Pierre

■ Patriotic ceremony behind Saint-Étienne church late afternoon on the 9th of July in the presence of the Allies and the Free French Forces from the Scamaroni Company.

■ Caen, Place Monseigneur-des-Hameaux. Stele commemorating the ceremony on the 9th of July

■ Following over a month-long siege, the Canadians finally enter Caen on the 9th of July

■ Saint-Étienne church and the Abbaye-aux-Hommes (now the town hall), which was home to the Lycée Malherbe in 1944, provided shelter for thousands of refugees during the siege of Caen

■ Refugees in Saint-Étienne church

left Caen, some in a massive southward exodus, others to hide in the underground quarries such as those at Fleury-sur-Orne. But between 10,000 and 15,000 people stayed put, most of them seeking refuge in the western part of the town, spared from the bombs under the roof of Saint-Étienne church, the various buildings of the Abbaye-aux-Hommes (Men's Abbey) or the annexes of the Bon Sauveur psychiatric hospital.

Many monuments pay tribute to the liberators, the Canadian 3rd Division and the British 3rd Division. Others have been erected in memory of civilian victims. Finally, tribute is also paid to the Resistance, particularly the 70 or 80 misfortunate prisoners summarily executed by the Gestapo on the morning of the 6th of June.

AD PERPETUAM MEMORIAM   EN PERPETUELLE MEMOIRE

ANNO DNI MCMXLIV FIDE MUNITI ET EXEMPLO	L'AN 1944, PENDANT LA BATAILLE LIBÉRATRICE,
RR. DD. LEONIS GOURDIER DES HAMEAUX	LES CAENNAIS, SOUTENUS PAR LEUR FOI ET
PAROCHI HUJUS ECCLESIAE ROBORATI	L'EXEMPLE DU CURÉ-DOYEN DE SAINT-ETIENNE,
CIVES CADOMENSES INSTANTE PUGNA PRO	LÉON GOURDIER DES HAMEAUX, ONT ABRITÉ
LIBERTATE IN HAC ORATIONIS DOMO VITAM	LEUR VIE ET LEUR ESPÉRANCE SOUS LES
ET SPEM SUAM IN TUTO COMMISERUNT	VOÛTES DE CETTE ÉGLISE

■ Plaque – «In perpetual memory»

■ Refugees crowded into Saint-Étienne church, part of the Abbaye-aux-Hommes

Caen at a glance

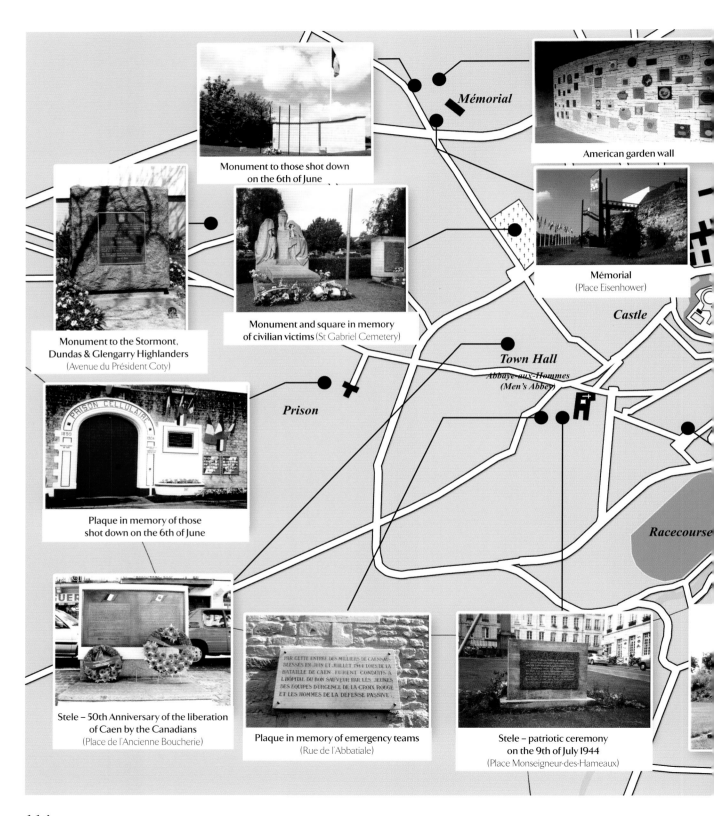

Monument to those shot down
on the 6th of June

American garden wall

Mémorial

Mémorial
(Place Eisenhower)

Castle

Monument to the Stormont,
Dundas & Glengarry Highlanders
(Avenue du Président Coty)

Monument and square in memory
of civilian victims (St Gabriel Cemetery)

Town Hall

Abbaye-aux-Hommes
(Men's Abbey)

Prison

Plaque in memory of those
shot down on the 6th of June

Racecourse

Stele – 50th Anniversary of the liberation
of Caen by the Canadians
(Place de l'Ancienne Boucherie)

Plaque in memory of emergency teams
(Rue de l'Abbatiale)

Stele – patriotic ceremony
on the 9th of July 1944
(Place Monseigneur-des-Hameaux)

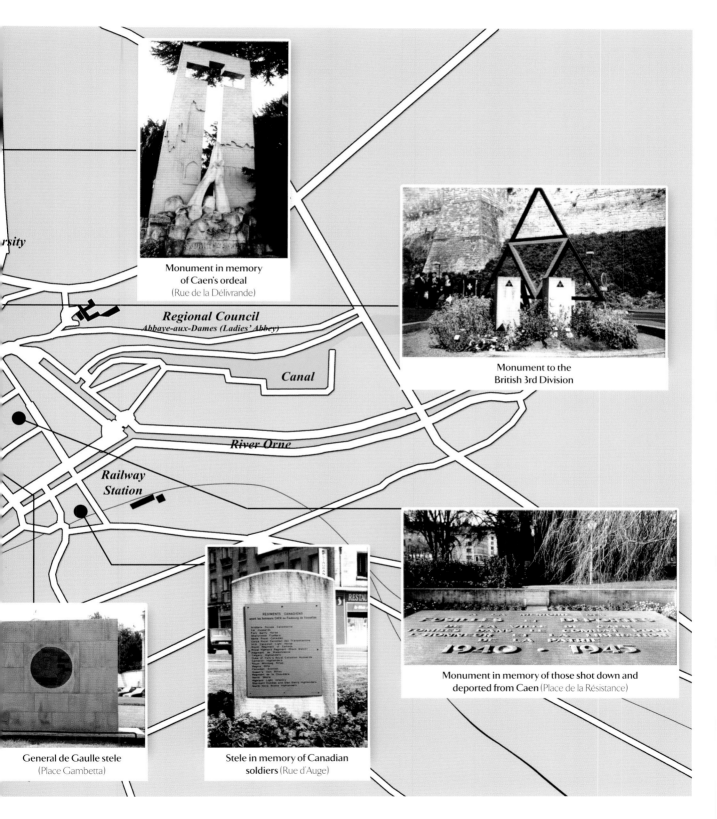

Monument in memory
of Caen's ordeal
(Rue de la Délivrande)

Monument to the
British 3rd Division

University

Regional Council
Abbaye-aux-Dames (Ladies' Abbey)

Canal

River Orne

*Railway
Station*

General de Gaulle stele
(Place Gambetta)

Stele in memory of Canadian
soldiers (Rue d'Auge)

Monument in memory of those shot down and
deported from Caen (Place de la Résistance)

■ Horsa gliders

Between the Orne and the Dives

The British airborne troop sector

To the east of the Orne estuary stretches an area of low-lying country touching the Caen plain and the Dives marshland, which was voluntarily flooded by the Germans in 1944. The men of General Gale's 6th Airborne were to drop here during the night of the 5th to the 6th of June. Their essential mission consisted in digging into this zone to protect the left flank of the sector, from which the Allies were to launch their daybreak assault, from German counter-offensives

117

■ Insignia of the
British paratroops

■ The day before the offensive. General Gale talking to the men of the 6th Airborne

Some groups were given precise objectives. For example, a series of bridges over the Dives and its tributary the Divette, at Troarn, Bures, Robehomme and Varaville had to be destroyed to prevent the rapid intervention of the units of the German 15th Army in position to the east of the river. On the other hand, the two interconnecting bridges at Ranville and Bénouville crossing the Orne and the canal had to be captured intact. They were the only means of crossing from one bank to the other between Caen and the sea, and would enable the troops coming from Sword Beach to bring their support rapidly to the airborne troops. This delicate mission was entrusted to the 2nd Battalion "Ox and Bucks" (Oxford and Buckinghamshire Light Infantry) under Major Howard, who crossed the Channel aboard six Horsa gliders. Simultaneously, a parachute batta-

lion was to capture the battery at Merville, whose four supposedly 150mm guns it was feared would cause serious damage on the nearest landing beaches.

In spite of all these difficulties, and frequently demonstrating valiant courage the «Red Berets» achieved all

the tasks that had been assigned to them. Meanwhile, the main part of the 6th Airborne landed on Norman soil shortly before one in the morning, not without some losses. Many men became lost, some even falling straight into the marshes. Around half past three a first wave of gliders brought fresh troops and heavy weaponry. Another followed at the end of the day. A defensive perimeter was set up around the bridges of Ranville and Bénouville to contain the first German counter-offensives and the first

■ "The Channel stopped you, but not us..."

reinforcement commandos from Ouistreham reached there in the early afternoon, thus ensuring the junction with the 6th Airborne. Reinforcements from the 51st Scottish Division were soon to follow.

Violent fighting for possession of the ridge running from Sallenelles to Troarn took place over the following days, notably around Amfreville and Bréville. Then the front settled down and a long and exhausting war of position began, a war of patrols and raids under artillery bombardment and mortar fire. Operation Paddle was to be launched from this narrow bridge-head to the east of the Orne in mid-August, at the same time as the Germans were being surrounded in the Falaise pocket. The offensive drive to the Seine was launched by a very cosmopolitan army including British and Canadian troops, the Belgian Piron Brigade, the Dutch Princess Irene Brigade, and the Frenchmen from Kieffer's unit.

■ Paratroopers in defensive position at a crossroads near Ranville.

■ German fortifications near the Baie de Sallenelles

Bénouville

■ Pegasus Bridge in British hands. Horsa gliders in the background, just a few yards from the bridge.

On the 6th of June at 0015 hours the three Horsa gliders carrying Major Howard's men achieved the feat of landing just a few yards from the bridge at Bénouville. Small stone blocks on the small path that runs along the canal mark the exact spot where each glider drew to a halt. A bronze bust of Major Howard has been erected near the first of these.

The element of surprise had its full effect and the raiders managed to capture the bridge. hardly firing a shot. With reinforcements from the paratroopers. they were required to hold on to the position and repel German counter-attacks. notably from the 21st Panzer. until the arrival of the first Commando brigade at about one in the afternoon. Contrary to the legend. Bill Millin stopped playing his bagpipes. so as not to draw unwanted enemy fire. when he crossed the bridge with Lord Lovat. This first success on a day that was full of them has secured world renown for the modest village of Bénouville and its bridge. the now legendary Pegasus Bridge.

On the Major John Howard Esplanade. beside the Landing Committee signal monument. there is a plaque dedicated to the «Ox and Bucks» and the German anti-tank gun whose mission was to defend the bridge.

On the opposite bank. the famous Gondrée café. the «first house in France to be liberated in the last hour of the 5th of June» as a plaque affixed to its façade proudly

■ Bust of Major Howard

The Pegasus memorial, which opened in June 2000, lies between the canal and the Orne and its historic space encompasses the venerable Bénouville Bridge, which was dismantled in 1993 due to new navigational requirements on the canal and replaced with a slightly larger «twin brother». A Horsa glider, rebuilt to its identical state, is also displayed in the park.

■ The legendary Gondrée café «the first French house to be liberated»

■ Stele recalling the first Bailey bridge to be built across the canal to reduce the bottleneck at Pegasus Bridge

states, has become a favourite rendezvous for the veterans of the 6th Airborne every D-Day anniversary. For its part, the town hall prides itself in being the first in France to have been liberated... on the 5th of June at 2345 hours. Sceptical observers are reminded that, at the time, there was a difference between British time, French time (of which there were in fact two: the old and the new) and, not forgetting, German time which had been imposed at the beginning of the occupation, hence complicating the equation... and facilitating exaggeration.

Bénouville and Ranville bridges being unable to cope with all the traffic between the two banks, the British engineers launched the construction of several metal bridges both upstream and down. They were dismantled in the autumn to be used elsewhere. Around 400 yards from the Gondrée café towards Caen along the canal-side path, a stele recalls the existence of one of these structures called «London Bridge», which was the first Bailey bridge to be built in France, three days after the invasion.

■ Reinforcements entering Bénouville

Ranville

■ A few dozen yards now separate the new Bénouville Bridge from its venerable predecessor, Pegasus Bridge, that is now housed in the Ranville museum

While Major Howard's men were busy capturing Bénouville Bridge a few hundred yards away, Lieutenant Fox and his troop captured the swing bridge over the Orne at Ranville without difficulty, its guards losing no time in taking to their heels. «Horsa Bridge» never achieved the prestige that its neighbour did. Nevertheless, a stele indicates the conditions in which it was captured by the crew of the two gliders that managed to set down nearby (a third having become lost nearly twenty miles away).

The paratroops of the 5th Brigade captured, without meeting with further resistance, the village that can thus, and rightfully, pride itself on being the «first village in France to be liberated». A plaque on the wall of a broad field, where the gliders carrying the heavy weaponry landed a short while later, indicates that it was by then 0230. We will not make any more of that here, given the problem of the time differences already mentioned. In any case, General Gale established his HQ in Ranville during the night. Gale was commander of the 6th Airborne and a bronze bust in his likeness now stands near the town hall, at the entrance to the municipal library.

Most of the paratroopers who fell victim to the fighting on the 6th of June and the following weeks were buried in the Ranville military cemetery, alongside a few hundred German soldiers. There are, however, some graves in the village cemetery right beside it. There lies Lieutenant «Den» Brotheridge, fatally wounded as he led his men in

■ The swing bridge at Ranville

middle of the month of August and shared in the liberation of the Calvados coast from Cabourg to Honfleur. At the foot of the old mill, the town of Ranville has erected a memorial paying tribute to Major Strafford, who devoted his whole life to ensuring the perpetuation of the memory of his comrades'

the charge on the bridge at Bénouville. He was without doubt the first Allied soldier killed in the fighting in Normandy. On the Place Général Gale, on a low wall opposite the entrance to the military cemetery, a series of panels explains the operations undertaken by the 6th Airborne on the 6th of June. Not far from there, a plaque on the side of a former mill recalls the participation of the Belgian soldiers in the final part of the Battle of Normandy. The brigade commanded by Colonel Jean Piron, which became part of the British 2nd Army, joined the fighting in the

■ The grave of Lieutenant Brotheridge, the first Allied soldier to be killed in Normandy

■ Bust of General Gale, Commander of the 6th Airborne

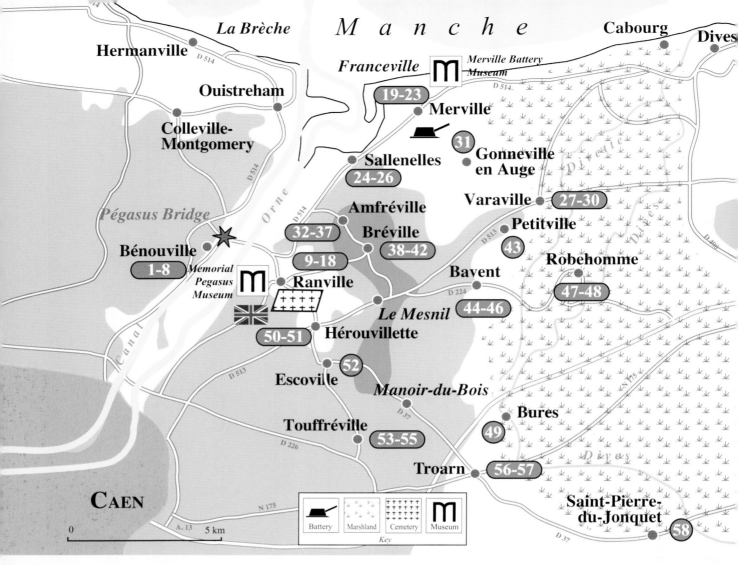

BENOUVILLE
1. Bust of Major Howard
2. Stones marking the places the gliders landed
3. Plaque - 2nd Battalion Ox & Bucks
4. Landing Committee signal monument
5. Plaque - first house liberated (Café Gondrée)
6. Plaque - first town hall liberated
7. Monument to the 7th Parachute Battalion
8. Stele - first Bailey bridge built in France

RANVILLE
9. Stele - Horsa Bridge (bridge)
10. Horsa glider (museum)
11. Brigadier Hill's statue
12. Plaque - first village liberated in France
13. Plaque - Lieutenant Brotheridge (village cemetery)
14. Wall with plaques recounting operations on 6th June
15. Major Stafford memorial (mill)
16. Plaque – Scottish paratroopers (mill)
17. Plaque – Belgian Piron Brigade (mill)
18. Bust of General Gale (library)

MERVILLE-FRANCEVILLE
19. Stele - 9th Parachute Battalion (battery)
20. Bust of Lieutenant-Colonel Otway (battery)
21. Monument to N°45 Royal Marines Commando
22. Stele - Belgian soldiers from the Piron Brigade (town hall)
23. Memorial to the liberators and civilian victims (Poste Office)

SALLENELLES
24. Monument to the 4th Special Service Brigade
25. Plaque - first Belgian soldier killed in France
26. Monument to the Belgian soldiers from the Piron Brigade

VARAVILLE
27. Memorial to the 1st Canadian Parachute battalion
28. Stele - N°3 Commando
29. Stele - 3rd Parachute Squadron of the Royal Engineers
30. Stele - Piron Brigade (Le Hôme)

GONNEVILLE-EN-AUGE
31. Stele - 9th Parachute Battalion

Amfreville
32. Stele - N°6 Commando (village centre)
33. Commando plaque (commando farm)
34. Monument to the 1st Special Service Brigade (church)
35. Monument to N°3 Commando (le Plain)
36. Monument to N°4 Commando (le Hauger)
37. Stele – 4th Brigade (le Hauger)

BRÉVILLE
38. Stele - 6th Airborne
39. Stele - Battle of Bois-des-Monts (Saint-Côme Castle)
40. Monument to the 51st Highland Division (Saint-Côme Castle)
41. Stele - Captain Ward and Private Masters (cemetery)
42. Stele – Princess Irene Brigade

PETITVILLE
43. Stele - N° 3 Commando

BAVENT
44. Stele - Brigadier Hill's 3rd Parachute Brigade (Le Mesnil)
45. Monument to the 1st Commando Brigade (village centre)
46. Stele on Brigadier Mills Roberts' tomb (cemetery) liberators of the village

ROBEHOMME
47. Plaque - Canadian 1st Parachute Battalion (church)
48. Plaque – Engineers and 1st Canadian Parachute Battalion (Bailey bridge)

EURES
49. Stele - 3rd Parachute Squadron of the Royal Engineers (bridge)

HÉROUVILLETTE
50. Plaque - 2nd Battalion Ox & Bucks (cemetery)
51. Pegasus Trail milestone (east town exit)

ESCOVILLE
52. Stele – British troops

TOUFFRÉVILLE
53. Stele - 8th Battalion of the Parachute Regiment (Manoir du Bois)
54. Stele - Brigadier Pearson (Manoir du Bois)
44. Stele - Privates Platt and Billington

TROARN
56. Stele - Major Roseveare (Saint-Samson Bridge)
57. Plaque - 3rd Parachute Squadron of the Royal Engineers

SAINT-PIERRE-DU-JONQUET
58. Monument to those shot down

Merville - Franceville

■ The Merville battery

The Germans had installed a series of secondary defensive positions east of the Orne estuary.

Many remains of these fortifications are still to be found on the beach and in the Varaville dunes, near an old 18th Century fort. The artillery in this sector, 47 or 50mm, hardly posed a threat to the troops who were to attack on the other side of the river, because of their insufficient range.

On the other hand, the battery situated south of the small town of Merville, further inland, with its four bunkers housing – according to the British intelligence report – 150mm guns, constituted a genuine menace that the aerial bombardments could not be sure of annihilating. Consequently, it was decided to capture it the night before the invasion. Lieutenant-Colonel Otway's 9th Parachute Battalion trained intensely for the mission to capture this fortified position, surrounded by minefields and barbed wire and defended by a garrison of nearly 150 gunners, but nothing went as planned.

Due to the very wide-ranging dispersal of his men during the drop, Otway only managed to assemble 150 or so, deprived of most of their material, instead of the 600 originally making up his unit. Moreover, the three gliders that were to have landed inside the defensive perimeter were nowhere to be seen. Nevertheless, they launched the assault. And yet, after a furious battle, which resulted in heavy losses in the ranks of the attackers and left very few survivors on the German side, their objective was attained.

The battery was in British hands shortly before 0500 hours. The successful assailants were surprised to discover that the guns were less powerful than had been thought. They were in fact of a calibre of 100mm which, although capable of reaching Sword beach, did not present a major threat to the landing operation.

This does not diminish the fact that the capture of the Merville battery constitutes one of D-Day's great feats of arms. A museum established in a former bunker tells the story of this heroic deed. At the entrance to the site, a stele has been erected in tribute to the 9th Parachute Battalion. A bronze bust immortalises the determination of its commander, Lieutenant-Colonel Otway

Amfreville

■ Amfreville, June 1944. The French marine fuseliers from N°4 Commando back with their compatriots

The village of Amfreville, liberated on the evening of the 6th of June, became the meeting place and the HQ of the various units constituting Lord Lovat's 1st Special Service Brigade, including Lt. Commander Kieffer's French marine fuseliers. These units defended the north of the bridge-head against German attacks to the east of the Orne. Alongside the paratroopers, during the days following D-Day, the commandos notably repelled powerful offensives launched by the 346th Division, which had been sent from its base in Rouen.

Commemorative monuments are particularly numerous here. At the entrance to the village of Amfreville - Le Plain, in front of the

■ The monument to N°6 Commando, erected in front of the «Commandos' farm»

«Commandos' Farm», a stele pays special tribute to N°6 Commando. Further on, in front of the church, on the Place du Commandant Kieffer, a very early monument, inaugurated as early as July 1944, is dedicated «to the memory of the officers and men of the 1st Special Brigade who lost their lives in the fight for Normandy». Erected around the same time, the little monument to N°4 Commando is located on the Place du Colonel Dawson (commander of the unit) on the hillock at Oger (or Hauger), a hamlet at the edge of the village on the way to Sallenelles. The stele to N°3 Commando, which dates from the 55th anniversary of the invasion, has been erected near the town hall.

■ Monument to N°4 Commando.
Erected in July 1944, in the midst of battle and with whatever lay at hand (it was moulded in a washing basin),
this small monument is the oldest of all those commemorating the events of summer 1944. It is conceived in the Scottish tradition, a cairn made with as many stones as there were men in the Commando unit;
177 of them symbolise Lieutenant commander Keiffer's French combatants

■ Ceremony on the 14th of July 1944 before the church and the monument to the 1st Special Brigade.

Bréville

■ Monument ot the 5lst Scottish Division

The Germans had established strongholds on the Bréville heights, positions that dominated and threatened the British. They had, therefore, to be captured. The village, which was taken by the commandos on the 7th of June and devastated by the bombardments, was lost to a counter-offensive. On the 11th of June, reinforcements in the form of the Black Watch Regiment of the Scottish 5lst Division, which had just arrived on the bridgehead, were given a severe thrashing and had to retreat.

A renewed assault on the evening of the 12th of June launched by the paratroopers finally succeeded in dislodging the Germans, with heavy losses on both sides. Bréville was in British hands, but the castle of Saint-Côme, perched on a neighbouring hill, was to remain a no-man's land that both camps wrestled over until August. The memorial erected at Bréville crossroads pays tribute to the men who captured the village and notably to the 162 airborne troops killed during the clash, including Colonel Johnson, the commander of the 12th Parachute Battalion. Near Saint-Côme castle several monuments paying tribute to the 9th Parachute Battalion, the 51st Scottish Division and the Dutch troops from the Princess Irene Brigade recalls the fighting in that sector, now referred to as the Battle of Bois-des-Monts.

■ Stele in memory of the men from the 6th Airborne Division who lost their lives during the liberation of Bréville

Troarn

Over three-quarters of the little market town of Troarn was destroyed by the fighting there before it was liberated on the 17th of August. In the very first hours of the 6th of June, it had been the scene of a particularly spectacular event. The destruction of the Saint-Samson bridge, at the edge of the village on the road to Dozulé, was part of the mission assigned to the 3rd Parachute Squadron of the Royal Engineers, who dropped just before 1am... 6 miles away, near Ranville. Its commander, Major Roseveare, sending the rest of his men on foot in the direction of the other bridges over the Dives, took charge of the operation personally. Piled onto a jeep towing a trailer full of explosives, with nine sappers and an officer, they set off for Troarn. At the entrance to the village, a guard was imprudently killed by a burst from a machine gun, with the result that the whole garrison came out into the main street. Roseveare and his heavy material ran a hellish gauntlet of fire through Troarn, accelerator to the floor, losing en route one of their men, who was thrown from the vehicle, on the way. The descent towards the Dives enabled them to gain speed and get out of range. At 0520 hours, the bridge blew. Today, a stele recalls Major Roseveare and his men's feat. For his part, Captain Juckes managed to destroy the two bridges at Bures in the same manner at around 0930 hours. A memorial pays tribute to this young officer who was killed in fighting some weeks later.

■ The team with which Major Roseveare managed to destroy the bridge at Saint-Samson was very probably similar to this one

Saint-Pierre-du-Jonquet

The monument in Saint-Pierre-du-Jonquet pays tribute to the 28 local inhabitants who were savagely executed by the Nazis during the Battle of Normandy. Most of them were arrested for having helped the British paratroopers that had become isolated following the bad drops on the night of the 5th to the 6th of June. They were taken to Argences, to where the Caen Gestapo had retreated, and were subjected to vicious torture before being executed without trial. Their bodies, hastily thrown into bomb craters not far from there in Saint-Pierre-du-Jonquet, were discovered after the war. Eleven of them were unidentifiable. They now lie in a square in the village cemetery. It is possible that the bodies of other victims the Gestapo murdered in similar circumstances have never been found.

■ Monument to those shot down by the Gestapo

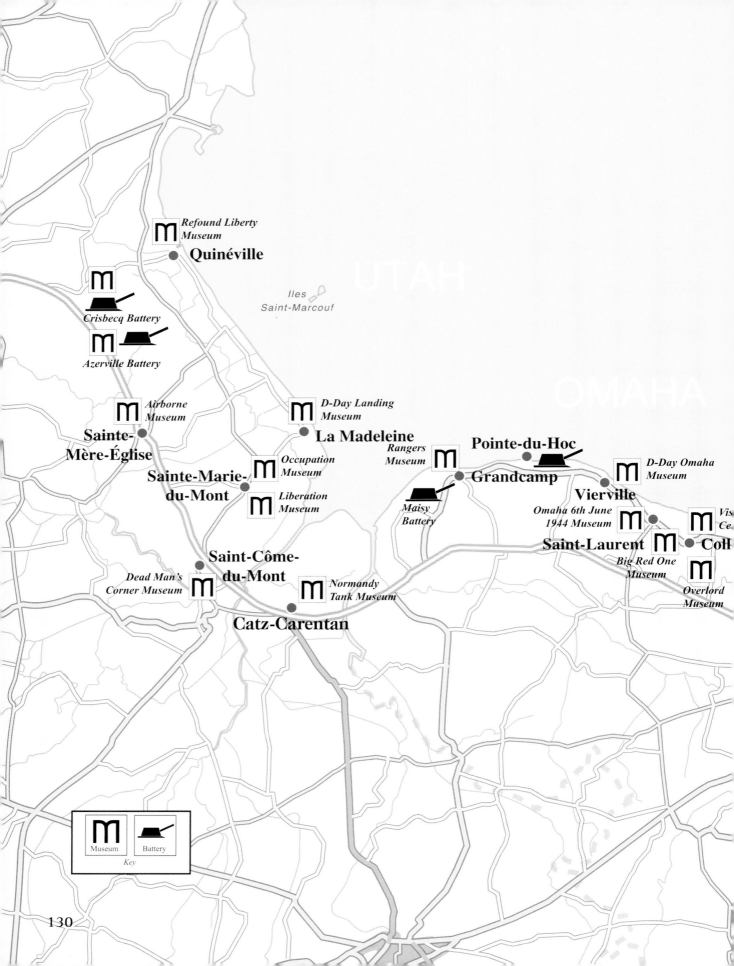

Refound Liberty
Museum

Quinéville

*Iles
Saint-Marcouf*

UTAH

OMAHA

Crisbecq Battery

Azerville Battery

*Airborne
Museum*

*D-Day Landing
Museum*

**Sainte-
Mère-Église**

La Madeleine

*Occupation
Museum*

*Rangers
Museum*

Pointe-du-Hoc

*D-Day Omaha
Museum*

**Sainte-Marie-
du-Mont**

*Liberation
Museum*

Grandcamp

Vierville

*Maisy
Battery*

*Omaha 6th June
1944 Museum*

Saint-Laurent

Vis
Ce

Coll

*Big Red One
Museum*

**Saint-Côme-
du-Mont**

*Dead Man's
Corner Museum*

*Normandy
Tank Museum*

*Overlord
Museum*

Catz-Carentan

M	⬛
Museum	Battery

Key

D-Day
Landing Museums

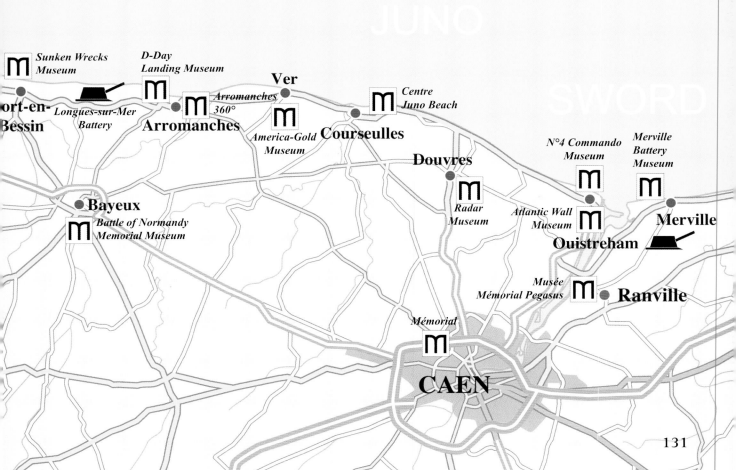

GOLD

JUNO

SWORD

Sunken Wrecks Museum

D-Day Landing Museum

Ver

ort-en-Bessin

Longues-sur-Mer Battery

Arromanches

Arromanches 360°

America-Gold Museum

Courseulles

Centre Juno Beach

Douvres

Radar Museum

N°4 Commando Museum

Atlantic Wall Museum

Ouistreham

Merville Battery Museum

Merville

Bayeux

Battle of Normandy Memorial Museum

Musée Mémorial Pegasus

Ranville

Mémorial

CAEN

131

PHOTO CREDITS

Calvados Departmental Archives: : 44(bl), 5I(b), 79, 83(b), 92(I), 96(b), II3(t), II4-II5, I29(b).

Canadian National Archives : II(b), 8I(r), 82, 83(t), 86-87(b), 88(t), 89(t), IIO, III(b), 4e couv.

Bundesarchiv Coblence : 6(b), 8, 56(t), 95(r), I04(bl).

DIREN : 93(tr).

Editions Normandes Legoubey : 2I(b), 23, 29, 36-37, 45(b), 5I(t), 70(m), 75(t), 77(t), 92-93(b).

Imperial War Museum, Londres : IO, I3(tr), 63(r), 64(t), 65, 66(b), 67(b), 69(b), 70(t), 72, 77(bd), 9I(t), 96(t), 97(t), 99(t), I00-I0I(b), I0I(hl), I06(t and c), I07(t), II2(b), II3(b), II7(r), II8, II9(t and bl), I20(t), I2I(tr and br), I23(tl), I26(t), I27(b), I29(t).

Jean-Luc Leleu : 79.

Delphine Leneveu : II4.

Caen Memorial : couv, 7(t), 44(t), 6I(tr), 68(t), 73(t), 75(br), 98(b), I05(I), I07(c and b), I09, II4-II5, I2I(tl).

Airborne Museum, Saint-Mère-Église : 23.

Michel DEHAYE : 4-5, I6-I7, 36-37, 62-63, 75(h), 80-8I, II6-II7, I22 (h), http://avuedoiseau.piwigo.com

Washington National Archives : couv, 5(r), I2, I3(hl), I7(r), I8, I9, 22(t and bl), 26(tr and bl), 27(b), 28, 30(t), 32(tl and c), 34(t), 35(t and c), 37(r), 38, 39, 40(b), 4I(b), 43(t and bl), 45(t), 48(b), 49(t), 50(b), 52, 55(r), 57(tr and b), 60(t), 6I(tl), 7I, 74(b), 4e couv.

ONAC Calvados (Julia Quellien : 4-5, 42(c), 46-47, 48(t), 49(b), 53(b), 56(b), 57(tl and c), 58-59, 60(c), 6I(b), 69(tr), 70(b), 7I(bl), 77(bl), 79, 86(tl), 87(tr), 97(b), I04(t), II4-II5, I23(br).

OREP : 2-3, 9(b), 33(t), 54-55, 80-8I, 89(t), 94-95, II2(t), I22, I25(t).

Jean Quellien : 6(t), 7(b), 9(t), II(t), I3(b), I6-I7, 2I(t), 22(br), 23, 24, 25, 26(tl and br), 27(t), 29, 30 (b), 3I, 32(tr), 33(b), 34(c and b), 35(hr and b), 42(b), 43(br), 46-47, 50(t), 53(t and c), 58-59, 62-63, 68(b), 69(tl and m), 7I(hl and br), 74(t), 75(bl), 76, 78, 79, 83(c), 85, 86(tr), 87(tl), 88(c), 89(b), 90, 9I(b), 92(tr), 93(c and br), 98(t), 99(b), I0I(tr and m), I02, I04(br), I05(b), I06(b), I08, III(t), II4-II5, II6-II7, II9(br), I20(bl),I2I(m), I23(m and bl), I25(b), I26(b), I27(t and c), I28.

OREP EDITIONS

Zone tertiaire de NONANT - 14400 BAYEUX
Tél.: 02 31 51 81 31 - **Fax:** 02 31 51 81 32
E-mail: info@orepeditions.com - **Web:** www.orepeditions.com

Graphic design and layout: OREP

ISBN : 978-2-915762-70-9 - Copyright OREP 2010